Criminal Justice
Recent Scholarship

Edited by
Marilyn McShane and Frank P. Williams III

A Series from LFB Scholarly

Risk Factors in Computer-Crime Victimization

Kyung-shick Choi

LFB Scholarly Publishing LLC
El Paso 2010

Library of Congress Cataloging-in-Publication Data

Choi, Kyung-shick, 1973-
    Risk factors in computer-crime victimization / Kyung-shick Choi.
        p. cm. -- (Criminal justice: recent scholarship)
    Includes bibliographical references and index.
    ISBN 978-1-59332-401-8 (hbk. : alk. paper)
    1. Computer crimes. I. Title.
    HV6773.C4778 2010
    364.16'8--dc22

                                        2010014561

ISBN 978-1-59332-401-8

Printed on acid-free 250-year-life paper.

Manufactured in the United States of America.

Table of Contents

Acknowledgments

I thank the reviewers and editors of this book: Dr. Marilyn McShane, Dr. Frank Williams, and Leo Balk. I would like to thank Dr. Dennis Giever at Indiana University of Pennsylvania for offering his thoughtful guidance and ensuring adequate quality of my research work. I wish to thank, Dr. Daniel LeClair, at Boston University, for his encouragement, continuous emotional support and helpful advice for my academic career. I would like to extend a special thanks to Dr. Jake Gibbs, who offered constant kind encouragement and allowed me to conceptually and operationally build a strong analytical foundation. Without having them, I would have been unable to reach my goal of being a criminology scholar. I was greatly inspired pedagogically by both professors.

CHAPTER 1

Introduction and Overview of Computer Crime

Everyday aspects of our lives are performed at the leading edge of technology, as society depends heavily on computer technology for almost everything in life. The rapid development of technology is also increasing the dependency on computer systems. Perhaps, we are currently living in two separate worlds: the physical world and the cyber-world. Even the level of connectedness with which people can be connected via high-speed Internet has altered the way we socialize. Individuals receive services, search for information, exchange customized text messages, and pay bills with a mobile phone browser. People are connected and socialize with others visiting video-chatrooms and online games sites in cyberspace.

Thus, cybercrime has the potential to affect everyone's daily activities. Today, computer criminals are using this increased dependency on technology as a prime opportunity to engage in illicit or delinquent behaviors. It is almost impossible to have precise statistics on the number of computer crimes and the monetary loss to victims because computer crimes are rarely detected by victims or reported to authorities (Standler, 2002). In addition, policing in cyberspace is very minimal at best (Britz, 2004). Moreover, computer criminals are becoming more sophisticated in their criminal behavior. Cybercrime has become a real threat to the quality of life. Few people have recognized the overall impact of computer crime. More importantly, people do not realize how they are constructing their online lifestyles through the constant usage of computer technology.

PURPOSE AND SCOPE

This book is intended to introduce patterns of computer-crime victimization by applying routine activities theory. Rather than capturing all forms of computer crimes, this book mainly focuses on individual victimization based on computer virus incident. This shall be done by presenting the argument that Cohen and Felson's (1979) routine activities theory is actually an expansion of Hindelang, Gottfredson, and Garofalo's (1978) life-exposure theory. One of the main concepts from life-exposure theory, lifestyle variables, is arguably what Cohen and Felson refer to in routine activities theory as their target suitability component. These lifestyle variables contribute to potential computer-crime victimization. The concept of interest is an individuals' daily pattern of routine activities, including vocational activities and leisure activities, in cyberspace that increase the potential for computer-crime victimization. Also of importance is one of the three major tenets from routine activities theory, "capable guardianship." The tenet of interest is how computer security, as an important capable guardian in cyberspace, plays a major role against computer-crime victimization.

The intended audience for this book includes anyone who is interested in learning details regarding computer crime, the causes of individual computer crime victimization, and computer crime research. Error! Bookmark not defined.Cohen and Felson's (1979) routine activities theory and Hindelang, Gottfredson, and Garofalo's (1978) lifestyle-exposure theory have been widely applied to explain various causes of criminal victimization, and the results have delineated victims' behavioral patterns that correspond with the victims' vulnerability to crime. However, the research of these two theories reveals that no empirical studies, among the 100 studies examined from the Internet development period from 1989 to 2006, have focused on computer-crime victimization. Most crime categories in these studies consisted of violent crime and property crime.

Even though there are a number of surveys focusing on computer crime without taking theoretical perspectives into consideration, the studies predominately focus on computer crime against business, with an obvious absence of focus on individual computer-crime victimization (Moitra, 2005). Thus, this project produces contributes in a significant way to the empirical literature in criminology, as this book focuses on private individual computer-crime victimization via a theoretical approach using routine activities theory. A structural equation model (SEM) is used to assess the new theoretical model advanced in this book by providing an overall picture of the relationship among the latent variables in the proposed model.

COMPUTER CRIME AND VICTIMIZATION

Most people are confused about the difference between cybercrime and computer crime. In fact, some cybercrime authors do not appropriately separate the use of the terms. Therefore, before looking into the details on computer-crime victimization, it is necessary to define the difference between cybercrime and computer crime.

Casey (2001) defines cybercrime as "any crime that involves computers and networks, including crimes that do not rely heavily on computers" (p. 8). Thomas and Loader (2000) also note that cybercrime is "computer-mediated activities which are either illegal or considered illicit by certain parties and which can be conducted through global electronic networks" (p. 3). Basically, cybercrimes cover wide categories of crime in cyberspace or on the World Wide Web including, "computer-assisted crimes" and "computer-focused crimes" (Furnell, 2002, p. 22).

In general, special computer operating skills are not required to commit cybercrime. For example, a suspect and a victim may communicate via Web based chat-rooms, Microsoft Network messenger (MSN), or e-mail. Once the criminal gains the potential victim's trust, the criminal is in the position to commit a crime against the victim. In this case, even though the Internet probably assisted the suspect in communicating with the victim, it does not mean that the technology or the Internet caused the crime (Casey, 2000). Indeed, in computer-assisted crimes, a computer does not have to play a major role in the crime. It can merely be the tool that is used by the suspect that assists in facilitating the eventual offense such as in the case of fraud or in a confidence scam.

According to Casey (2000) the more general term cybercrime can be contrasted with computer crime or computer-focused crime, special types of cybercrime. Specifically, these refer to

> a limited set of crimes that are specially defined in
> laws such as the US Computer Fraud and Abuse Act
> and the UK Computer Abuse Act. These crimes
> include theft of computer services; unauthorized
> access to protected computers; software piracy and
> the altercation or theft of electronically stored
> information; extortion committed with the assistance
> of computers; obtaining unauthorized access to
> records from banks, credit card issuers, or customer
> reporting agencies; traffic in stolen passwords and
> transmission of destructive viruses or commands.
> (pp. 9-10)

Since manipulation of digital data is considered as one of key ingredients in computer crime, these computer crimes usually require more than a basic level of computer-operating skill for offenders to commit these crimes successfully against victims. In fact, offenders who commit a cybercrime or a computer crime are both contacting this new place, cyber-space, which is a realm different from the physical world, and which has different jurisdictions and different laws that we can apply.

In this study, the individuals committing illegal or unwanted invasions of someone else's computer, including the implantation of viruses, are referred to as "computer criminals," because the project focuses solely on computer-crime victimizations. Indeed, the focus of this research is on individual victimization through computer crimes, particularly computer hacking, which can include the implantation of computer viruses. The term "hacking" originally referred to access by computer experts, who love to explore systems, programs, or networks in order to identify computer systems' vulnerabilities and develop ways to correct the problems (National White-Collar Crime Center, 2003). However, the term "hacking" currently, and more correctly refers to unauthorized access with "intent – to cause damage, steal property (data or services), or simply leave behind some evidence of a successful break-in" (National White-Collar Crime Center, 2003, p. 1).

The number of individuals victimized by computer crimes has increased annually (Gordon, Loef, Lucyshyn, & Richardson, 2004). Flanagan and McMenamin (1992) state computer crimes committed by a new generation of hackers might cost cybercrime victims, as a collective, anywhere from $500 million to $5 billion a year. The Computer Emergency Response Team Coordination Center (CERT/CC) reports that "the number of reported incidences of security breaches in the first three quarters of 2000 has risen by 54% over the total number of reported incidences in 1999" (McConnell International LLC, 2000, p.1). This suggests that the hacker world is rapidly changing for the worse. Kabay's (2001) summary of studies and surveys of computer crime estimated that losses to victims of virus infections reached approximately $7.6 billion in the first half of 1999. Moreover, according to the 2005 CSI/FBI Computer Crime and Security Survey, virus attacks continue to effectuate the most substantial financial losses and, compared to the year 2004, monetary losses have significantly escalated due to "unauthorized access to information" and the "theft of proprietary information" (Gordon et al., 2004, p. 15). The most recent 2008 CSI survey indicated that the average monetary loss per respondent (organization) based on computer security incidents was decreased from $345,005 in 2007 to $288,618 in 2008. However, the monetary loss is still high compared to the loss of $167,713 in 2006, and 49% of respondents' organization has reported their virus incidents. The 2008 IC3 also reported that the total dollar loss based on the total 275,284 complaints of crime linked to Internet fraud cases was $265 million, an increase of $239.09 million in total reported losses in 2007.

Unfortunately, the general population has still not recognized the overall seriousness of computer crime. This may explain, in part, an individual's online lifestyle patterns and the lack of computer security that can both significantly increase criminal opportunities for computer criminals in cyberspace. In addition, Kubic (2001) argues that law enforcement agencies are unable to catch up with recent technology to investigate various computer criminal cases, and the way the Department of Justice deals with cyber-offenders, especially hackers, appears to be quite lenient due to the absence of adequate laws regarding computer crime. However, the good news is that the law enforcement agencies have recently begun to focus on high-tech crime, and the Department of the Justice has begun to bring numerous criminal prosecutions throughout the country against individuals and groups engaging in various types of computer and cybercrime. Today, law enforcement is more frequently involved in the area of computer crime using government regulation, supported by the best federal bureaucracies with their large staff and monetary resources. Agents of the Bureau of Immigration and Customs Service, the Secret Service, and the FBI have major roles in international cybercrime investigations with support from the federal government. Federal regulatory agencies with specific cybercrime investigation and information security-related contracts include the Federal Aviation Administration (FAA), the Federal Communications Commission (FCC), the Federal Deposit Insurance Corporation (FDIC), the Federal Elections Commission (FEC), the Security Exchange Commission (SEC), and the U.S. Nuclear Regulatory Commission (MacQuade, 2006). In addition, the Cyber Security Enhancement Act was enhanced with additional components of the USA PATRIOT Act of 2001, and the law adjusted sentencing guidelines in the case of cybercrime, including punishments imposed on first-time and chronic computer criminals. In 2002, the creation of the Department of Homeland Security (DHS) unified existing federal agencies such as the U.S. Coast Guard, U.S. Secret Service, the Immigration and Naturalization Service (INS) inclusive of the U.S. Border Patrol, and the FBI's National Information Protection Center (NIPC) for counterterrorism, including IT-enabled crimes (MacQuade, 2006).

CRIMINOLOGICAL FOUNDATIONS ON COMPUTER CRIME VICTIMIZATION

Both Hindelang et al.'s (1978) lifestyle and Cohen and Felson's (1979) routine activities theories were espoused during the same period of time that the criminal justice system began to place value on studying victimization issues (Williams & McShane, 1999, pp. 233-234). Criminologists in the early 1970s began to realize the importance of victimization studies because they previously placed their focus on the criminal offender and ignored the crime victim (Karmen, 2006). Creation of "the self-report survey" and the emergence of national victimization studies in 1972 facilitated the development of victimization theories in this era (Karmen, 2006, p. 51). Lifestyle-exposure theory and routine activities theory were introduced based on the evidence of "the new victimization statistics" as a part of a rational theoretical perspective embedded in sociological orientation (Williams

& McShane, 1999, p. 235). The two theories appear to be ideally suited for understanding why individuals are predisposed to crime and how an individual's activities, interactions, and social structure provide opportunities for offenders.

Hindelang et al. (1978) suggest that an individual's daily patterned activities, such as vocational and leisure activities, contribute to victimization. They posit that an individual's expected social roles and social position influence their personal lifestyle patterns, and contribute to the individual's decision to engage in certain activities. More importantly, engaging in risky activities can be made through individual rational choice.

Cohen and Felson (1979) assume that there are three main components to predict a likelihood of an occurring victimization event. First, a motivated offender must exist for the victimization to occur. Second, the presence of a suitable target is necessary for the occurrence of the victimization. Third, the absence of a capable guardian makes easy access for offenders to victimize the target. There must be a confluence or convergence of all three components for the victimization to occur. Thus, absence of one of the three components is likely to decrease or eliminate the victimization occurrence.

In this study, lifestyle variables from lifestyle-exposure theory, which arguably equates to the level of target suitability in routine activities theory, and the capable guardianship variable from routine activities theory are taken into account. This project hypothesizes that an individual's computer-oriented lifestyle in cyberspace contributes to his or her potential computer-crime victimization. In addition, the study also hypothesizes that the presence of installed computer security in a computer is a significant factor that can prevent or minimize the occurrence of computer crimel.

Thus, the purpose of this book is to explain the causes of computer-crime victimization via specific components from traditional victimization theories (lifestyle theory and routine activities theory) at a microlevel. This will be accomplished by examining the individual's online lifestyle, including properly updating and measuring any installed computer security programs.

CHAPTER 2

Computer Crime Victimization and Criminological Perspectives

Although cybercrime has rapidly evolved and become a significant criminological issue, research reveals that academia has developed a few significant empirical assessments regarding computer-crime victimization and the potential contribution to this victimization by online users' characteristics combined with their lack of computer security components. Therefore, the main purpose of this chapter is to discuss two traditional victimization theories, routine activities theory (Cohen & Felson, 1979) and lifestyle-exposure (Hindelang, Gottfredson, & Garofalo, 1978) theory, and their potential application to computer-crime victimization by examining the theoretical core concepts within these theories. Arguably, these two theories are actually one theory, with Hindelang et al.'s (1978) theory being expanded upon by Cohen and Felson in 1979. These two theories have been, individually, widely applied to various crimes, as discussed below, and they have attempted to tie primary causations of victimization to demographic factors, geographic difference, and traits of lifestyle.

ROUTINE ACTIVITIES THEORY AND NATURE OF CYBERSPACE

In 1979, Cohen and Felson proposed their routine activities theory,which focuses mainly on opportunities for criminal events. Cohen and Felson posited that there are three major tenets that primarily affect criminal victimization. The main tenets are (a) motivated offenders, (b) suitable targets, and (c) the absence of capable guardians against a violation (Cohen & Felson, 1979; Cohen, Felson, & Land, 1980; Felson, 1986, 1988; Kennedy & Forde, 1990; Massey, Krohn, & Bonati, 1989; Miethe, Stafford, & Long, 1987; Roneck & Maier, 1991; Sherman, Gartin, & Buerger, 1989). The researchers argued that crime is likely to occur via the convergence of the three tenets. In other words, lack of any of the suggested tenets will be sufficiently capable to prevent a crime occurrence (Cohen & Felson). Other criminologists, namely Akers (2004) and Osgood et al. (1996) noted that routine activities theory suggests that most crimes are associated with the nature of an individual's daily routines based on sociological interrelationships; thus, illustrating that crime is based on situational factors which enable the criminal opportunities.

Yar (2005) applied the routine activities theory core concepts and "aetiological schema" to computer crime in cyberspace (p. 1). Even though Yar's study does not provide an empirical assessment, it guides the current project to construct an optimum measurement strategy by clearly defining new conceptual definitions in computer crime and traits of cyberspace that reflect the core concepts of routine activities theory. Therefore, this section will focus on two phases that reflect Yar's (2005) research. In the first phase, spatiality and temporality in cyberspace are presented, while comparing these items to crimes in the physical world. In the second phase, the major tenets of routine activities are presented via the application of computer crime.

Spatiality and Temporality in Cyberspace

Cohen and Felson (1979) emphasized the importance of "the spatial and temporal structure of routine legal activities" that facilitates an interpretation of how criminals take opportunities to transfer their criminal inclinations into criminal acts (p. 592). In other words, an individual's daily activities in a social situation produce certain conditions or opportunities for motivated offenders to commit criminal acts. Utilizing burglary as an example, frequent social activities away from home can facilitate increasing criminal opportunity, as the absence of a capable guardian at home is likely to make household property a suitable target (Garofalo, 1987).

Indeed, many studies support the likelihood of property crime victimization as being associated with frequent absences from the home (Corrado et al., 1980; Gottfredson, 1984; Sampson & Wooldredge,

1987; Smith, 1982). Routine activities theorists also argue that crime victimization can be determined by a "proximity to high concentrations of potential offenders" (p. 596; see Lynch 1987; Cohen et al., 1981; Miethe & Meier, 1990). However, the important question is how to link from these concepts in the physical world to computer-crime victimization in cyberspace.

In order to apply the concept of routine activities to the computer-crime issue, cyber-spatial and cyber-temporal structures need to be defined. Cyberspace or online activities consist of Web sites hosted by digital communities ("chat rooms," "classrooms," "cafes," etc.) that link together via the World Wide Web (Adams, 1998, p. 88-89). The significant difference between physical-space and cyberspace is that, unlike a physical location, cyberspace is not limited to distance, proximity, and physical separation (Yar, 2005). Mitchell (1995) referred to cyberspace and its environment as "antispatial" (p. 8). Stalder (1998) also asserted that the cyber environment is composed of a zero-distance dimension. Clicking a digital icon in cyberspace takes an online user everywhere and anywhere. Thus, the mobility of offenders in cyberspace far exceeds the mobility of offenders in the physical world. Although it has been proposed that the mobility rules of the physical world would not apply in the world of cyberspace (Dodge & Kichin, 2001; Yar, 2005), this would only necessarily apply in dealing with the weight or physical bulk of the target.

Examining social context factors in both physical and cyber-spatial structures is crucial because social environments interact with the traits of spatiality, and this association can provide criminal opportunities. In the physical world, numerous studies suggest that social context factors have a substantial influence on crime victimization. The National Crime Survey and British Crime Survey have consistently indicated that demographic factors such as age, race, and marital status are associated with general crime victimization (Cohen et al., 1981; Gottfredson, 1984, 1986; Laub, 1990). Cohen and Cantor (1980) specifically found that the demographic characteristics associated with a typical larceny victimization include "a family income of $20,000 or more a year, sixteen through twenty-nine year olds, people who live alone, and persons who are unemployed" (p. 140). Mustaine and Tewksbury (1998) examined minor and major theft victimization among college students and found that the victims' demographic factors, types of social activities, level of self-protective efforts, neighborhood environments (level of noise), and the participation in illegitimate behaviors (threats with a weapon) have a strong influence on the level of both minor and major theft victimization risk.

Bernburg and Thorlindsson (2001) expanded routine activity theory, referring to it as "differential social relations," by mainly focusing on social context that addresses situational motivation and opportunity. The study was based on cross-sectional data from a national survey of Icelandic adolescents. Bernburg and Thorlindsson (2001) found that a routine activities indicator, "unstructured peer interaction in the absence of authority figures," is positively associated with deviant behaviors (violent behavior and property offense), and the association between the routine activities indicator and deviant behavior is significantly accounted for by social contextual factors (pp. 546-547).

Cyberspace also shares a common social environment with the physical world. Castells (2002) asserted that cyberspace is oriented from the social and international environment in our society and reflects the "real world" of socioeconomic and cultural dimensions (p. 203). In other words, cyberspace is "real space'" that is closely correlated to the physical world. Internet users can view diverse Web pages everyday as a part of their routine activities in relation to their different needs. Online users with different demographic backgrounds may visit different types of Web sites based on their different interests and, thus, the compilation of a cyber-community can be distinguished by its members' interests in cyberspace (Castells, 2002).

In addition, even though there are no limitations on physical distance in order to connect another place in cyberspace, Internet users usually find a popular Web site (i.e., Ebay, MSN, AOL, Myspace.com) that has a higher density of Internet connections than other domains via a search engine (i.e. Google, Yahoo). Therefore, a higher density of Internet connection may indicate the proximity of computer criminals and computer-crime victims (Yar, 2005). In fact, computer victimization occurrences can be seen in many social networking Web sites.

In terms of the concept of temporarily, routine activities theory assumes that a crime event occurs in a particular place *at a particular time*, which indicates the importance of a clear temporal sequence and order for a crime to occur. Cohen and Felson (1979) asserted that "the coordination of an offender's rhythms with those of a victim" facilitates a convergence of a potential offender and a target (p. 590). In Cohen and Felson's proposition, crime occurrences in particular places may be applicable to a study of computer-crime victimization because computer criminals often search suitable targets in certain social networking sites where online users are populated (Piazza, 2006). However, their proposition of a particular time does not seem to match with the temporal structure of cyberspace. The uniqueness of the temporal structure of cyberspace is that computer users and crime offenders are globally populated because the World Wide Web does not limit time zones and is fully available to anyone at anytime for access (Yar, 2005). Thus, it is almost impossible to estimate the number of computer criminals that are engaging in crimes at any specific point in time. However, just as is noted in routine activities theory, it is assumed that there is always a motivated offender waiting for the opportunity to commit a criminal act.

THREE CORE CONCEPTS: ROUTINE ACTIVITIES THEORY

Motivated Offender: Computer Criminal

The routine activities theoretical perspective suggests that there will always be a sufficient supply of crime motivation, and motivated offenders are a given situational factor (Cohen & Felson, 1979). This project accepts Cohen and Felson's assumption that there will always be motivated offenders. Therefore, the new computer-crime victimization model will not test this specific element, but it is important to explain the computer criminals' motivations and why the existence of motivated offenders in cyberspace is a given situation in this research.

The Internet has allowed certain people to find new and innovative ways to commit traditional crimes. These people are called "hackers." The term "hacker" was originated from a tradition of creating attention-seeking pranks (called "hacks") at the Massachusetts Institute for Technology (MIT) in the 1950s and 1960s (Wark, 2010). Hacking was achieved among computer enthusiasts for recognition via improvements or modifications to each other's programming code (Wark). Hackers form computer clubs and user groups, circulate newsletters, attend trade shows, and even have their own conventions. More recently, the term has changed to have negative connotations, referring to those who use computers for illegal, unauthorized, or disruptive activities (Knetzger and Muraski, 2009). In order to emphasize this difference, some use the term "cracker" to refer to the latter and "hacker" as it originally was used (Wark, 2010). Britz (2004) described hackers as people who view and use computers as toolkits of exploration and exploitation. In fact, there has been very little research on the way how they truly operate in cyberspace. Holt (2009) argues that hackers have become engaged in various criminal activities such as cyber terrorism and organized crime but the prevalence of these criminal groups within hacker subculture is unknown.

Hoffer and Straub's (1989) study of the motivations of computer abusers indicated that 34.1% of the hackers abuse computer systems for their personal gain, 26% of hackers do so for fun and entertainment purposes, 11.4% of the hackers intentionally attack computer systems, and 28.4% of the hackers misuse computer systems due to ethical ignorance. According to the 2004 Australian Computer Crime and Security Survey (2005), 52% of respondents from the survey believed that the primary motive of the computer criminals was "unsolicited malicious damage" against their organization, while other respondents believed that the computer criminals are motivated by "the possibility of illicit financial gains or commercially motivated sabotage" (pp. 14-15).

Computer criminals use computers, and telecommunications links, as a potentially dangerous and costly deviant behavior, partially for the purpose of breaking into various computer systems (Britz, 2004). They also steal valuable information, software, phone services, credit card numbers, and digital cash. They pass along and even sell their services and techniques to others, including organized crime organizations (Britz, 2004). In cyberspace, motivated computer criminals are online to find the suitable targets (online users), who connect to the Internet without taking precautions or using computer security software (Britz, 2004).

Thus, in cyberspace, motivated offenders and suitable targets collide frequently. Grabosky (2000) lists the most evident motivations of computer criminals as "greed, lust, power, revenge, adventure, and the desire to taste 'forbidden fruit'" (p. 2). After an Internet Technology employee is fired from a company, the angered employee may retaliate by shutting down the company's computer systems. Computer criminals, like "cyber-punks," want to try hacking to have fun, and they like to feel in control over others' computer systems (Britz, 2004). After getting caught by authorities, they often claim that they were just curious. In addition, "crackers" implant a malicious virus to a computer system, or take valuable files which may contain customer information such as credit card numbers or social security numbers (Britz, 2004). They can then sell or illegally use the information, thus posing a threat to corporate security and personal privacy (Rosenblatt, 1996).

Parker (1998) also described computer criminals' motives as greed, need, and the inability of recognizing the harm towards computer-crime victims. In addition, Parker (1998) asserts that computer criminals tend to utilize "the Robin Hood syndrome" as their justification for committing crimes. Therefore, following Cohen and Felson's (1979) theoretical assumption in terms of motivated offenders, the suggested various research also speculates that motivated offenders are a given situational factor. This is due to the fact that computer criminals, with various motivations, are available in cyberspace. Thus, one of routine activity theory's tenets, motivated offenders, nicely matches with motivated computer criminals.

Suitable Target in Cyberspace

The second tenet, a "suitable target" refers to a person or an item that may influence the criminal propensity to commit crime (Cohen, Kluegel, & Land, 1981; Felson, 1998). So, theoretically, the desirability of any given person or any given item could be the subject of a potential perpetuator (Cohen et al., 1981; Felson, 1998). However, crime victimization is mostly determined by the accessibility dimension, which links to the level of capable guardianship, regardless of the target desirability (Cohen et al., 1981; Yar, 2005).

Felson (1998), in an extension to the theory, presented four different target suitability measures based on the potential offender's viewpoint. Felson referred to the offender's perception of the *value* of target to likely offender, the *inertia* of the target to likely offender, the *visibility* of the target to likely offender, and the *access* to easily exit from the offense location (commonly referred to as VIVA). First, the valuation of targets becomes complicated in computer crime because the complexity is associated with the offender's motivation or purpose to commit computer crime (Yar, 2005). Even though Hoffer and Starub's research (1989) and the 2004 Australian Computer Crime and Security Survey briefly delineate a computer criminal's motivation (for malicious intent, personal pleasure, personal gain, etc.) toward computer-crime victims, it is difficult to conclude that the research reflects the true estimate of the computer criminal's motivation. This is due to the fact that the survey respondents, company employees, do not represent the pool of the computer criminal population. In fact, many criticisms on computer crime related quantitative and qualitative research are driven from lack of "generalizable data" based on computer-crime incidents against private victims in quantitative research, and small sample sizes in qualitative research that may draw biased outcomes (Moitra, 2005).

However, research indicates that one of clearest computer criminals' targets are individuals, or an organization, from whom they seek to obtain digital property. This is because cyberspace is formed by digital codes that contain digital information and digital property (Yar, 2005). Digital property such as business Web sites and personal Web sites can also be vandalized by computer criminals, or the criminals can steal important personal information such as social security numbers or credit cards numbers (Yar, 2005). Thus, the targets in cyberspace can experience a wide range of offenses committed against them including trespass, theft, cyber stalking, or vandalism based on the potential offender's intent (see Bernburg & Thorlindsson, 2001; Birkbeck & LaFree, 1993; Yar, 2005).

The second measure of VIVA, the inertia of crime targets, is an important criterion in target suitability. Inertia and suitability have an inverse relationship; a higher level of the inertial resistance is likely to weaken the level of the target suitability (Yar, 2005). In human-to-human confrontations, it may be more difficult for the offender to commit a violent crime against a physically stronger target (Felson 1998; Felson 1996). Comparatively, in cyberspace, the level of inertia of crime targets may be affected by "the volume of data" if the computer criminals have limited computer systems such as a very low capacity in their hard drive, their memories, or their CPUs (Yar, 2005). However, overall, the inertia of a crime target in cyberspace is relatively weaker than the physical world because the cost of computers is becoming affordable and the development of technology constantly helps computer criminals equip themselves with more efficient tools, such as high-speed Internet and external hard drives, to commit computer crimes.

The third measure of VIVA, the visibility of crime targets, has a positive association with target suitability (Bennett, 1991; Felson, 1998; Yar 2005). That is, the level of target visibility increases the crime target suitability. Since most computer-crime targets in cyberspace are intangible, consisting of digital information, it would be difficult to conceptualize its visibility (Yar, 2005). However, computer criminals gain the digital information from online users through various toolkits they can use in cyberspace, such as I.P. Trackers or Password Sniffers. Therefore, the gained valuable digital information such as credit card information, personal documentation, or passwords, is observable via a computer monitor. Such information can then be transformed to a hard copy via a printer. Thus, computer-crime targets are "globally visible" to computer criminals in cyberspace (Yar, 2005).

The fourth measure of VIVA, accessibility, has a positive correlation with target suitability. Felson (1998) defined accessibility as the "ability of an offender to get to the target and then get away from the scene of crime" (p. 58). The IC3 2004 Internet Crime Report (2005) indicated that one of the most significant problems in investigating and prosecuting computer crime is that "the offender and victim may be located anywhere worldwide" (p. 13). In fact, the Internet provides criminals with vast opportunities to locate an abundance of victims at a minimum cost, because computer criminals use computers to cross national and international boundaries electronically to victimize online users (Kubic, 2001).

In addition, the sophistication of computer criminal acts, by the criminals utilizing anonymous re-mailers, encryption devices, and accessing third-party systems to commit an offense for the original target, makes it difficult for law enforcement agencies to apprehend and prosecute the offenders (Grabosky 2000; Grabosky & Smith 2001; Furnell, 2002; Yar, 2005). Thus, anonymity and sophistication of computer criminal techniques in cyberspace strengthens the level of accessibility that provides computer criminals with the ability to get away in cyberspace.

In sum, the application of VIVA to cyberspace indicates that target suitability in cyberspace is a fully given situation. When an online user accesses the Internet, personal information in his or her computer naturally carries valuable information into cyberspace that attracts computer criminals. In addition, if computer criminals have sufficiently capable computer systems, the inertia of the crime target becomes almost weightless in cyberspace. The nature of visibility and accessibility within the cyber-environment also allows the motivated cyber-offenders to detect crime targets and commit offenses from anywhere in the world. Therefore, the current project speculates that within the three Routine Activities theoretical components, the most viable tenet that can control the level of computer-crime victimization is the level of capable guardianship.

Capable Guardianship in Cyberspace

In the third tenet of routine activities theory, an absence of capable guardianship, a guardian can simply be a person who can protect the suitable target (Eck & Weisburd, 1995). Guardianship can be defined in three categories: formal social control, informal social control, and target-hardening activities (Cohen, Kluegel, & Land, 1981). First, formal social control agents would be the criminal justice system, which plays important roles in reducing crime (Cohen et al., 1981). Examples of these formal social controls would be the police, the courts, and the correctional system.

In cyberspace, computer crime is likely to occur when online users have an absence of formal capable guardians. Law enforcement agencies contribute formal social control against criminals to protect prospective victims (Grabosky, 2000). Tiernan (2000) argued that primary difficulties in prosecuting computer criminals arise because much of the property involved is intangible and does not match well with traditional criminal statutes such as larceny or theft. This problem weakens the reliability of formal social control agents and is compounded by the increasing number of computer criminals who have been able to access both private and public computer systems, sometimes with disastrous results (Tieran, 2000).

As stated earlier, formal social control agencies have increasingly acknowledged the need to stress new priorities and promote innovative crime prevention strategies designed to counter the advent and continued growth of computer crimes (Taylor, et. al, 2006). Even though federal agencies have guided law enforcement efforts against computer crime, most state and local law enforcement officers still lack knowledge concerning the processing of computer data and related evidence which would be necessary for effective computer-crime investigations (Taylor, et. al, 2006). Hinduja (2009) argues that that the lack of resources and failure of dissimilation of updated technology and training within local and state enforcement agencies are significant impediments to combat against the catalyst of new forms of computer-related crime. Specialized forces to patrol cyberspace are very limited, and they seem to face an extreme difficulty in building a strong formal guardianship for online users (Grabosky, 2000; Grabosky & Smith, 2001). In addition, computer criminals are able to commit crime from any geographic location, and they target victims from all over the world (Kowalski, 2002). Furthermore, the rapid development of technology allows a computer criminal's identity to be concealed by using various computer programs, some of which are mentioned above, which make it very difficult to identify a suspect (Grabosky, 2000).

The 2005 FBI Computer Crime Survey (2006) revealed that computer-crime victims tend not to report incidents to law enforcement agencies for various reasons. The survey found that 23% of the respondents believed that law enforcement would not take any action against the crime, and an equal ratio of respondents believed that law enforcement does not have the ability to help prevent computer crime. The findings also indicate that the computer-crime victims are less likely to contact law enforcement agencies for assistance because of a lack of faith in the criminal justice system.

In the physical world, examples of informal social control agents would be parents, teachers, friends, and security personnel (e.g., see Eck, 1995; Felson, 1986). Informal social control involves groups of citizens and individuals who can increase the surveillance and protection function (Cohen, Kluegel, & Land, 1981). In cyberspace, informal social guardians range from "private network administrators and systems security staff" to "ordinary online citizens" (Yar, 2005, p. 423). Even though criminal justice policies have been slowly geared toward computer-crime initiatives to increase public awareness, by relying upon "self-regulation, codes-of-conduct or etiquettes, monitoring groups (against for example, child pornography), and cooperative measures by private and semi-public groups" in order to minimize computer crime, these initiatives are not yet fully viable (Moitra, 2005).

In other words, similar to formal social control, informal social control agents are not actively operative in our cyber society. In addition, it is almost impossible for both formal and informal social control agents to maintain existing effective guardianship since computer criminals have acquired "the ease of offender mobility and the temporal irregularity of cyber-spatial activities" (Yar, 2005, p. 423). Thus, the current study posits that both formal and informal social control agents have little impact on computer-crime victimization.

The last category of capable guardianship, target hardening, is associated with activities through physical security such as lighting on areas, using locks, alarms, and barriers which are good examples to reduce the incidence of property crime in the physical world (Tseloni et al., 2004). Various literatures support that increasing the level of target-hardening activities via physical security is likely to decrease victimization risk (Chatterton & Frenz, 1994; Clarke, 1992, 1995; Clarke & Homel, 1997; Laycock, 1985, 1991; Poyner, 1991; Tilley, 1993; Webb & Laycock, 1992). In cyberspace, physical security can be equivalent to computer security with a digital-capable guardian being the most crucial component to protect the computer systems from computer criminals.

Even though technology has generated many serious cybercrimes, it has also created defense systems, so called computer security, to reduce the opportunity to commit computer-related crimes. The failure of an individual to equip their personal computer with computer security, which can enhance the level of capable guardianship in cyberspace, can potentially lead to online victimization. Indeed, the absence of computer security significantly weakens the guardianship and facilitates computer criminals in committing crimes. Thus, this digital guardian, installed computer security, is likely to be one of the most crucial elements of a viable capable guardianship in cyberspace.

When computers are tied to modems or cables, a whole new avenue to potential attack is opened. Simple password protections become insufficient for users demanding tight security (Denning, 1999). Computer security programs, such as anti-hacking software programs, protect the systems against an online attack. The threat is reduced on the mainframe computer because of software incorporated to prevent one user from harming another user's computer by accidental or illegal access. Thus, today many corporations and computer users install software such as firewalls, antivirus, and antispyware programs, to protect computer systems against hackers. In addition, biometric devices such as fingerprint or voice recognition technology and retinal imaging enhance the protection against unauthorized access to information systems (Denning, 1999).

Unfortunately, computer security is never absolute and the only secure computer is one that has no contact with the outside world (Denning, 1999). In other words, the computer system will never be completely secured, so it is impossible to remove the opportunity for computer criminals to commit crimes. However, computer users can minimize the criminal opportunity by installing computer security, so they can hinder criminals from penetrating their computer systems. Thus, the current project includes installed computer security as the crucial key element of a capable guardian, from the perspective of routine activities Theory, which is transposable into the new computer-crime victimization model.

TARGET SUITABILITY REVISITED: LIFESTYLE-EXPOSURE THEORY

In 1978, Hindelang, Gottfredson, and Garofalo developed the lifestyle exposure model which focuses on the victims' daily social interactions, rather than concentrating on the characteristics of individual offenders or individual causal variables. Lifestyle-exposure theory holds that criminal victimization results from the daily living patterns of the victims (Goldstein, 1994; Kennedy & Ford, 1990). Hindelang et al. (1978) defined lifestyle as "routine daily activities" including "vocational activities (work, school, keeping house, etc.) and leisure activities" (p. 241). The current project interest in lifestyle-exposure theory is to assess online lifestyles by examining the individual's online vocational activities and leisure activities that may contribute to computer-crime victimization. This section briefly introduces the concepts of the original lifestyle-exposure theory. Then, the lifestyle-exposure theory is applied to online lifestyles, such as vocational activities and leisure activities in cyberspace, online risk-taking behavior, and properly maintaining installed computer security systems.

Hindelang et al. (1978) posited that the lifestyles of individuals are determined by "differences in role expectations, structural constraints, and individual and subcultural adaptations" (p. 245). In the first phase of the lifestyle exposure theoretical model, Hindelang et al. (1978) discussed how role expectations and social structure create constraints. They conceptualized "role expectation" as expected behaviors that are corresponded to cultural norms, which link with the individuals' "achieved and ascribed statuses" (Hindelang et al., p. 242). Hindelang et al. argued that an individual's age and gender are substantially associated with role expectations, because certain age and gender differences are expected to follow normative roles in American society. The researchers defined "structural constraints" as "limitations on behavioral options" which constantly deploy conflicts to individuals by corresponding with "the economic, familial, educational, and legal orders" (Hindelang, et al., p. 242). Research by Kennedy and Forde (1990) found that personal variables associated with the lifestyle, such as age, sex, marital status, family income, and race, significantly influence daily activities and the level of criminal victimization risk. The study also suggests that lifestyle factors significantly reflect the individuals' amount of exposure time in places associated with victimization risk (Kennedy & Forde, 1990).

An adaptation process occurs when individuals or groups initiate gaining knowledge of skills and attitudes in order to manage the constraints associated with role expectations and social structure. This process develops some individual traits, including the individual's attitudes and beliefs. In the course of continuing these processes, the individuals modify their attitudes and beliefs, and these learned traits naturally become a part of the daily routine behavioral patterns (Hindelang et al., 1978). In the second phase of the model, differential lifestyle patterns are associated with "role expectations, structural constraints, and individual and subcultural adaptations (Hindelang et al.).

Hindelang et al. (1978) addressed the importance of the relationship between victimization and vocational and leisure activities. Vocational and leisure activities are the daily activities that are central to a person's life. These lifestyle activities are predictive of personal interactions with others as formal roles. Hindelang et al. asserted that lifestyle and exposure to the level of victimization risk are directly related in the model. Moreover, Hindelang et al. (1978) suggested that association, which refers to the level of personal relationships within individuals who share common interests, is another factor that indirectly links exposure to personal victimization. In other words, personal associations increase level of the exposure to individual victimization.

So, how can we define lifestyle activities in cyberspace? Like the physical world, in cyberspace, online users have online daily activities, such as checking e-mail, seeking information, purchasing items, socializing with friends, and obtaining online entertainment, which are becoming a major portion of the users' lives. Through online activities in cyberspace, people can constantly interact with others via various online tools, such as e-mail and electronic messengers, and create their own online lifestyle by engaging in various online communities based on their particular interests, such as cyber-cafés, clubs, and bulletin boards.

However, online lifestyles can result in a catastrophic event for online users. For instance, on May 3, 2000, many online users received and opened an e-mail from significant others, coworkers, or government officials with the subject line "ILOVEYOU" without sensing that the email was one of the most malicious viruses ever experienced by Internet users. The ILOVEOU virus was a fast-infecting virus that changed window registry settings and then e-mailed copies of itself to everyone in the original victim's Microsoft Outlook Express address book. Thus, clicking on the icon activated the virus. The virus then forwarded itself via e-mail to each address contained in the affected computer's Outlook address book (Winston Salem Journal, 2000).

Even though there was no clearly discernable, actual amount of monetary damage from the ILOVEYOU virus, the worldwide monetary damage due to the virus infection was estimated at between $4 billion to $10 billion, all occurring during a mere couple of days (Winston Salem Journal, 2000). This disastrous case clearly indicates that the Internet has become one of the most significant communication tools by combining online vocational and leisure activities into one method of "mail, telephone, and mass media" in cyberspace (Britz, 2004). The case presented above also illuminates that as digital necessity, in the form of going online, is becoming an increasing part of more peoples' lifestyles it is a crucial lifestyle activity that could also carry with it a very great threat to our personal lives.

Lifestyle-exposure theory attempts to estimate the "differences in the risks of violent victimization across social groups" (Meier et al., 1993, p. 466). It has been applied to various types of crime, and it has succeeded in various ways in explaining the causes of victimization (Meier et al., 1993). Gover (2004) tested victimization theories by utilizing a public high-school student population in South Carolina. This study suggested that the effects of social interaction indirectly influence violent victimization in dating relationships (Gover, 2004). Key factors were measured through risk-taking behaviors such as drug abuse, alcohol abuse, driving under the influence, and a promiscuous sexual lifestyle (Gover, 2004). The concept of risk taking factors can be applied to cyberspace.

In cyberspace, computer criminals attract online users through fraudulent schemes. In many hacking incidents, computer criminals typically attract a victim, and thus their computer systems, by offering free computer software, free MP3 music downloads, or free movie downloads. Various types of software such as Trojan horses, logic bombs, and time bombs are designed to threaten computer security, and many computer criminals use those viruses and worms by placing hidden virus codes in these free programs. Thus, clicking on an icon without precaution in social networking places in cyberspace can contribute to computer-crime victimization. According to the 2005 FBI Computer Crime Survey (2006), "the virus, worm, and Trojan category" was rated as the highest category of financial loss, which is a rate over three times larger than any other category (p. 10).

Like routine activities theory, life-exposure theory asserts that differential lifestyle patterns involve the likelihood of being in certain locations at certain times and having contact with people with certain characteristics. Thus, the occurrence of criminal victimization relies on "high risk times, places, and people" (Hindelang et al, 1978, p. 245). As noted in the routine activities theory section, temporality is not absolutely necessary in cyberspace because there is no time zone in cyberspace (Yar, 2005).

However, this proposed research argues that visiting certain locations in cyberspace may have a correlation with computer-crime victimization. In other words, specific lifestyle patterns directly link with "differences in exposure to situations that have a high victimization risk" (Hindelang et al, 1978, p. 245). Miethe and Meier (1990) asserted that physical proximity to perpetrators and the level of exposure is statistically associated with risky environment based on burglary, personal theft, and assault victimization cases. Their research used data from the British Crime Survey (Miethe & Meier, 1990). Kennedy and Forde (1990) also indicated that criminal victimization is not a random occurrence, but is strongly associated with certain geographic locations.

Computer criminals search for suitable victims in cyberspace. Online users congregate based on their interests, and they socialize with others in cyberspace. Piazza (2006) stated that computer users' information can be easily sent to hackers by simply clicking a pop-up window in "social networking sites" such as free download places and online bulletin boards when a hacker plants a malicious JavaScript code on these Web sites (p. 54). High levels of network activity on a particular site and search engine tools can guide offenders to popular Web sites in cyberspace (Yar, 2005). These popular Web sites become a sort of shopping mall for offenders, as they cause a multitude of potential victims to congregate in one localized area, thus enabling the offenders to shop for their potential targets.

In addition, properly maintaining installed computer security is a crucial factor in terms of online vocational activities. If an online user connects to the Internet without properly updating computer security, and visits the delinquent Web sites planted with computer viruses, it maximizes the risk of computer-crime victimization. Thus, the project also hypothesizes that those online users, who frequently visit the delinquent Web sites without precaution and neglect regularly updating installed computer security programs, have a high likelihood of experiencing computer-crime victimization.

POTENTIAL THEORETICAL EXPANSION

Both routine activities theory and lifestyle-exposure theory are widely applied to explain various criminal victimizations. In general, most studies found fairly strong support for both victimization theories with predatory and property crimes. Even though the two theories are empirically supported in the criminological research, the major critique resides in the failure of these theories to specify testable propositions regarding certain offenders' and victims' conditions, as such specification would allow for more accurate predictions of crime (Meier & Miethe, 1993). In addition, little research has been empirically tested on individual computer-crime victimization. Moreover, it is proffered here that routine activities theory is simply an expansion of the lifestyle-exposure theory espoused by Hindelang et al. in 1978. In other words, routine activities theory is really a theoretical expansion of lifestyle-exposure theory, as it adopts the main tenet in lifestyle-exposure theory, the individual's vocational and leisure activities. It appears that Cohen and Felson (1979) absorbed this tenet into what they call their suitable target tenet, and then add a motivated offender and a lack of capable guardianship. It is posited here that an individual's vocational and leisure activities are what makes him or her a suitable target. Even Cohen and Felson (1979) acknowledged this point. Cohen and Felson (1979) asserted that the individuals' lifestyles reflect the individuals' routine activities such as social interaction, social activities, "the timing of work, schooling, and leisure" (p. 591). These activities, in turn, create the level of target suitability that a motivated offender assigns to that particular target.

Thus, routine activities theory shares more than an important common theme with the lifestyle variable from lifestyle-exposure theory; it has actually incorporated this tenet and added the additional tenets of capable guardianship and motivated offender. This is akin to what Akers (1985) acknowledged that he did with Sutherland's (1947) differential association theory when he developed his social learning theory. Akers (1985) noted that he simply incorporated that theory into his theory by expanding upon the already existent differential association theory tenets. Hence, it is suggested here that these two theories, routine activities theory and lifestyle-exposure theory, are not two separate theories, but that routine activities theory is simply an expansion of lifestyle-exposure theory. Therefore, this study will apply routine activities theory while acknowledging that lifestyle-expansion theory provides a more complete explanation of the "suitable target" tenet found in routine activities theory.

From the routine activities theoretical perspective, one of three tenets, capable guardian, contributes to the new computer-crime victimization model in this project. This project assumes that motivated offenders and suitable targets are given situational factors. In cyberspace, pools of motivated computer criminals can find suitable targets in the form of online users who connect to the Internet without precaution or without equipping adequate computer security. The routine activities approach would lead to the practical application of situational computer-crime prevention measures by changing the conditions and circumstances.

This project finds that the most feasible method of preventing computer-crime victimization that can be adapted from routine activities theory is a target-hardening strategy. This is accomplished in the form of up-to-date, adequate computer security equipment. A target-hardening approach via computer security will make it more difficult for computer criminals to commit computer crimes in cyberspace. Since the operation of formal social control agents in cyberspace is very limited, establishing a viable target-hardening strategy can be made via equipping adequate computer security in the computer system. It is also of note that the individual can also increase the target-hardening strategy by updating and maintaining this computer security. However, updating and maintaining this computer security equates to the lifestyle choices made by the individual. Regardless of whether the person properly updates and maintains the computer security, the fact remains that equipping the computer with computer security is a crucial component in reducing computer criminal opportunities in the new theoretical model.

General research on the lifestyle-exposure theory is limited in explaining computer-crime victimization, but supportive of the new theoretical computer-crime victimization model. Although studies associated with lifestyle-exposure theory have not focused on computer-crime victimization, a victimology perspective based on a personal lifestyle measure under lifestyle-exposure theory is appropriate and useful for understanding computer-crime victimization. This is because the gist of the lifestyle-exposure theory is that different lifestyles expose individuals to different levels of risk of victimization. Thus, one of the research interests is to estimate the level of target suitability by measuring risk-taking factors that potentially contribute to computer-crime victimization. The project assumes that online users, who are willing to visit unknown Web sites or download Web sites in order to gain free MP 3 files or free software programs, or who click on icons without precaution, are likely to be victimized by computer criminals. In other words, the levels of online vocational and leisure activities produce greater or lesser opportunities for computer-crime victimization. Numerous findings support that lifestyle factors play significant roles in individual crime victimization in the physical world. This project hypothesizes that the level of online lifestyle activities would contribute to the potential for computer-crime victimization.

Hindelang et al. (1978) suggest that "vocational activities and leisure activities" are the most crucial components in a lifestyle which have a direct impact on exposure to the level of victimization risk. Here, the specific tenets from lifestyle-exposure theory, as expanded upon by routine activities theory, addressed herein as the online lifestyle activities measure, will be presented as an important theoretical component. In routine activities theory, Felson (1998) stated that target suitability is likely to reflect four main criteria: the value of crime target, the inertia of crime target, the physical visibility of crime target, and the accessibility of crime target (VIVA). This statement is a crucial point, which is compatible with the main lifestyle exposure theoretical perspective that explains why online users become suitable targets by computer criminals. It is the vocational and leisure activities that translate into the level of target suitability ascribed to Felson's (1998) VIVA assessment.

Mustain and Tewksbury (1998) argued that people who engage in delinquent lifestyle activities are likely to become suitable targets "because of their anticipated lack of willingness to mobilize the legal system" (p. 836). More importantly, the victims tend to neglect their risk of victimization by failing to inspect themselves regarding "where you are, what your behaviors are, and what you are doing to protect yourself" (Mustain & Tewksbury, p. 852). This study is designed to follow Mustain and Tewksbury's statement above.

The model is tested using SEM and is followed by a presentation of the research methods used in this study. The model actually consists of what is commonly referred to as two distinct theories, Cohen and Felson's (1979) routine activities theory and Hindelang et al.'s (1978) lifestyle-exposure theory. However, as shown above, routine activities theory is an expansion of lifestyle-exposure theory. Thus, routine activities theory's major concept, the target-hardening strategy, is represented by digital-capable guardianship. Hindelang et al.'s lifestyle-exposure theory's core concept, vocation and leisure activities, which is proffered here represents a more detailed explanation of the suitable target tenet in routine activities theory, is represented here by online lifestyle. This is done to estimate computer-crime victimization. The conceptual model posits that digital-capable guardianship and online lifestyle directly influence computer-crime victimization. This project also posits that convergence of the two variables has an interaction effect that contributes to a direct impact on computer-crime victimization.

Figure 1. *The conceptual model for computer-crime victimization.*

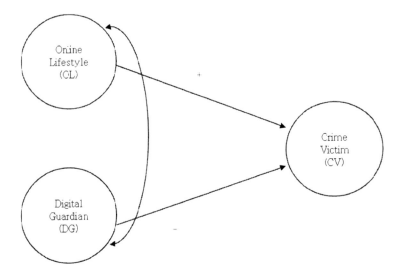

CHAPTER 3

Methodological Approach: Digital Guardian, Online Life Style, and Computer Crime Victimization

This chapter presents the research methods that are used to assess empirically the new computer-crime victimization model. This chapter includes sampling techniques, procedures, measures, hybrid model, measurement model, and the method of data analysis.

SAMPLE AND PROCEDURE

In the Spring 2007 semester, a self-report survey that contained items intended to measure the major constructs of cyber-routine activities measures was administered to university students in nine liberal studies classes at a university in the Pennsylvania State System of Higher Education (PaSSHE). This method permitted the researcher to select students from diverse majors randomly within the university. In order to avoid selecting the same students more than once, the notes on the first page of the survey form asked students not to take the survey again if they had previously participated in another class. In this way, the researcher would be able to reduce or eliminate duplicated student responses.

In addition, the study used a stratified-cluster, random-sample design. The sampling strategy consists of three steps. First, the full lists of liberal studies requirement classes that were available during spring 2007 were entered into a computer program known as the Statistical

Package for the Social Sciences (SPSS). Second, the lists of liberal studies requirements was stratified by class level (e.g., freshman: 100 level classes, sophomore: 200 level classes, and upperclassmen: 300 level classes and 400 level classes). Third, a proportionate subsample of classes was randomly selected by using SPSS. In essence, a list of the university's entire liberal studies requirement classes, the classes required for all students regardless of major, was entered into SPSS. The SPSS random number generator then randomly chose 10 of these general studies classes, based on class level, for inclusion in the sample. As noted by Maxfield and Babbie (2005), "the computer program numbers the elements in the sampling frame, generates its own series of random numbers, and prints out the list of elements selected" (p. 230). This sampling method ensured that it is a chance selection process. In other words, each of the general studies classes, based on class level, had an equal chance of becoming randomly selected for this study.

The researcher planned to obtain randomly a minimum of 172 completed surveys from the students for this study. The researcher derived the sample size by utilizing G*Power (a general power analysis computer program) based on an F-test in multiple regression analysis (Erdfelder et al., 1996). Entering 10 predictors (two observed variables from the digital-capable guardianship latent variable, three observed variables from online lifestyle latent variable, and three observed variables from online victimization latent variable, and two demographic variables) with a power of .95, and a medium effect size of $f = .15$, into the G*Power program computed the total sample ($N = 172$) at the .05 alpha level. Thus, threats to statistical conclusion validity were not an issue in this research. Surveying a minimum of 172 students allowed the researcher to have a large enough sample from which to assure that the sample size accurately represented the student population at the university.

In order to collect sufficient data the undergraduate population, 10 classes were sampled. Since the student size of individual liberal studies classes normally ranges from 20 students to over 100 students, selecting 10 classes from the total liberal studies requirements ensured generalizability to the undergraduate population, as this selection method ensured a large enough sample size from which to draw accurate generalizations to the population.

According to the university's Trendbook and Data Warehouse (2006), the freshman subsample, the sophomore subsample, and the upperclassmen subsample respectively consist of 34%, 22%, and 44% of the total university population of 12,047. Thus, randomly selecting 3 classes from the freshman sub-sample, 2 classes from the sophomore sub-sample, and 5 classes from the upperclassmen sub-sample generated a proportionate sample size that reflected each class level.

Table 1
Liberal Studies Requirements Sample

Class standing	Proportion of population Total liberal studies: 166 classes
Freshman	34% of 166 classes 34% of 10 (n) = 3 classes
Sophomore	21% of 166 classes 21% of 10 (n) = 2 classes
Upperclassmen	44% of 166 classes 44% of 10 (n) = 5 classes

Any student, who was enrolled in a general studies course and utilized his or her own personal computer, or laptop, was qualified to participate in this survey. This qualification was necessary because it would be extremely difficult to identify individual computer-crime victimization if the students only used public computers for their online activities. In addition, most students utilizing the public computers might be unaware of the security measures installed on those computers, thus affecting the accuracy of the measurements necessary for purposes of this study. Moreover, with a multitude of potential users for each of the public computers, one student's use of a computer might not be a proper measurement of the level of online risk engaged in by another student. Therefore, if a virus invaded that computer, the student experiencing the virus might not necessarily be the computer user who caused the opportunity for the virus to attack the computer.

Instructors who teach the selected general studies courses were asked for access to their classes in order to obtain the necessary number of participants in the study. Komorosky (2003) used a similar stratified cluster sample design and effectively obtained a representative sample of the undergraduate student population. This strategy, combined with the random sampling described above, enabled the researcher to make accurate and reliable statistical inferences from the random sample to the general undergraduate student population.

The survey instrument was used to delineate the big picture of computer-crime victimization patterns among the university student population. There were a couple of advantages in utilizing university students as the target sample for the proposed study. First, university students are expected to be literate and experienced in completing self-administered, self-report instruments. The university students are likely to produce high completion rates with a minimized measurement error compared to using different types of sample populations. Second, this researcher believes that, because of the reduction of costs of computers over the years and the fact that most students are required to submit typed work for their classes; the students are constantly using a computer for their work and entertainment. In addition, the younger generations are believed to be more likely to view a computer as a necessity of life than older generations are. This belief is supported by a study performed by the Internet Fraud Complaint Center (2003), which reported that younger generations are more likely to be victimized by computer criminals.

However, the sample had one obvious limitation. The researcher is purposely only selecting one university at which to conduct this study. If the sample does not represent the true college population, the findings may not be able to be generalized to the population of the college. Even if the sample does represent the true state college population, generalizability to other universities is still be a significant limitation because the results revealing the characteristics of the university sample may not accurately reflect the computer usage characteristics and levels of victimization experienced at the other universities. Thus, there is a limitation that arises regarding external validity. However, it is of note that the main purpose of this study is to assess routine activities theory to determine whether this theory will provide an explanation of computer-crime victimization.

Both the proposal and the questionnaire used in this research were reviewed and approved, prior to implementation, by the Institutional Review Board (IRB) at the university. In order to initiate the proposed research, after the IRB approval, the researcher asked the instructors in the classrooms for formal access to their classes to distribute the survey questionnaires to undergraduate students in their courses. Since gaining access to the classrooms was essential, a combination of sending a formal letter to each instructor, followed by personal meetings with the instructors, was used to increase the chances of gaining access. After the researcher received access to the classrooms with the instructors' permissions, the survey was administered to all the students in the classes who were present and willing to participate in the survey, and who utilized their own personal computer or laptop for the 10-month period of June of 2006 through and including March of 2007, with the exclusion of the students who already participated in the survey in another class.

The students who choose not to participate, or who were previously surveyed, were asked to sit quietly and patiently at their desks until the data collection period was concluded. In the voluntary consent form, the student's rights and guarantee of anonymity were stated. This statement was also read aloud to the students by the researcher. In this way, the researcher could adequately process the acquired data without any additional concern about violating the privacy of the participants.

RESEARCH HYPOTHESES AND MEASURES

The documentary film Hackers reports covering online users' vulnerabilities from their mischievous behaviors in cyberspace and computer security issues via hackers' and in both private and government computer security experts' in-depth interviews (Docherty, 2001). The survey instruments were inspired by the documentary film, and the specific measures that make up the assessment of the computer-crime victimization data were structured through the combined tenets from two known victimization theories: routine activities theory (Cohen & Felson 1979) and lifestyle-exposure theory (Hindelang, Gottfredson, & Garofalo 1978). The adopted theoretical components, as discussed earlier in the chapter 2, are capable guardianship and vocational and leisure lifestyles. Capable guardianship was measured in the form of digital-capable guardianship, represented by the number of installed computer security components and the duration of having the security. Lifestyles were measured in the form of online lifestyles, represented by individual online lifestyle behaviors. These theoretical component measures were analyzed in relation to their individual effects on the individual's overall computer-crime victimization. The survey was designed to collect data from a 10-month period. Students were asked to recall specific instances of computer-crime victimization for the 10-month period prior to participation in the survey. This would allow the researcher to estimate the computer-crime victimization during this period, which includes the spring, summer, and fall semesters at the university or at home, while providing for a short period from which the students have to recall any computer-crime victimization. The length of this recall period will minimize, or significantly reduce, any internal validity threats related to the participants' ability to recall accurately any incidents of computer-crime victimizations.

The suggested computer-crime victimization factors derived from the survey questionnaires contained the three major components that might facilitate computer-crime victimization. First, the level of digital guardianship in cyberspace was identified as the reason for the individual differences in equipping three crucial computer security programs in the student's computer. Therefore, this research hypothesized that the degree of installed major computer security programs differentiates the rate of computer-crime victimization. Second, this research also proposed that online vocational and leisure activities, online risky activities, and the management of cyber-security are the major observed variables that establish the victims' online lifestyles. Therefore, this research also hypothesized that online users who have risky online behaviors and a lack of management in computer security, such as adequately updating already installed computer security programs, combined with extensive hours online, are more likely to be victimized. Finally, the study posited that the convergence of the students' digital-capable guardianship and their online lifestyles has a significant impact on their individual computer-crime victimization.

DIGITAL GUARDIAN MEASURE

One of the major criticisms of routine activities theory is that a majority of the empirical tests on the theory only include indirect measures of suitable targets and capable guardianship, because they exclude measuring the presence of the motivated offenders (Akers, 2000).

However, as noted by Cohen and Felson (1979), there is always the presence of a motivated offender, and this would seem to be most especially true in the realm of cyberspace. As noted in the chapter 2, computer criminals are present in cyberspace and search for online victims anywhere and anytime. Thus, the research excluded any direct measures of motivated offenders from the proposed model because this study assumed that there will always be motivated offenders in cyberspace, just as Cohen and Felson (1979) suggested that there are always motivated offenders in the physical world.

In this research, measures of suitable targets from the original theory were also excluded. Following Felson's (1998) analysis of VIVA, the research here assumed that target suitability in cyberspace is also a given situation, albeit in varying levels and degrees. In other words, when an online user accesses the Internet, the criteria of target suitability (value, inertia of crime target, visibility, and accessibility) are met because being online conveys a sufficient condition, although at varying levels based on online lifestyles and activities, for the potential victimization in cyberspace. Thus, the researcher argues that one of the key components that this study derives from routine activities theory is the presence of a capable guardianship.

Yar (2005) suggested that formal social control agents do not seem to play important roles in minimizing computer-crime victimization. Yar also proposed that the absence of strong and effective law enforcement practices is likely to foster illegal computer criminal behaviors and limit the apprehension of computer criminals. Moreover, when they are caught, prosecution is very unlikely. However, digital-capable guardians, in the form of installed computer security systems, are capable of protecting against attacks from computer criminals. Moitra (2005) explained that potential computer-crime victimization occurrence involves "a high level of technology that is itself changing rapidly; the instrument of crime is generally intangible, usually being a string of digital signals; and the detection rates are exceptionally low, especially for Internet users who do not have a sophisticated detection system" (p. 456).

The three most common digital-capable guardians available to online users are antivirus software, firewalls, and antispyware. An antivirus program monitors a PC or laptop for computer viruses that might have gained an access through an infected e-mail message, a music download, or an infected floppy disk (Moore, 2005). If the antivirus computer software locates a virus, the software will attempt to remove it, or to isolate it, so the virus cannot continue to be a threat to the computer system. The most efficient antivirus programs constantly monitor your computer, scan incoming and outgoing e-mails, and run complete system scans every day (Moore, 2005).

A firewall program prevents intruders from accessing your computer over the Internet or a local network. The most efficient firewalls allow users, on a case-by-case basis, to stop malicious programs from connecting to the user's PC or laptop while the user is connected to the Internet. Moreover, firewalls may stop somebody from planting a virus, or worm, on the user's computer. However, firewalls do not detect or eliminate viruses (Casey, 2000).

Antispyware computer software is designed to prevent spyware from being installed in the computer system. Spyware is a computer software that collects the online users' personal information without gaining their informed consent (Ramasastry, 2004, p. 1). Spyware may collect various types of information. Some spyware attempts to track the Web sites a user visits in order to send this information to an advertising agency. More malicious spyware attempts to intercept passwords or credit card numbers that a user enters into a Web form or other applications (Ramsastry, 2004, p. 13).

This research posited that the absence of capable digital guardianship, in the form of installed computer security systems, would be the factor that would most likely allow vulnerability for computer criminals to attack, and equipping the digital guardians would be essential to minimizing the computer-crime victimization. The proposed study hypothesized that the number of installed security programs on a computer will differentiate the level or rate of computer-crime victimization. In other words, the proposed study hypothesized that the higher the number of installed security programs on a computer, the lower the level of computer-crime victimization. This study, as seen in Figure 2 below, directly measures the number of computer security equipment components in an online user's computer, in order to estimate the level of digital-capable guardianship.

Figure 2. *Digital guardian measures.*

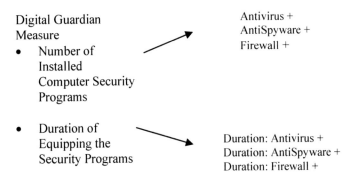

Digital Guardian
Measure
- Number of
Installed
Computer Security
Programs

Antivirus +
AntiSpyware +
Firewall +

- Duration of
Equipping the
Security Programs

Duration: Antivirus +
Duration: AntiSpyware +
Duration: Firewall +

As shown above, the digital guardian measure consists of two observed variables. The first observed variable consisted of three items based on three security programs. It was measured by asking the respondents to state what types of computer security they had in their own computer for the 10 months prior to participation in the survey. The three items based on this observed variable consist of dichotomous structure, which was identified 0 as absence of the specific computer security program and 1 as presence of the security. In other words, each scale was assigned a 1 for a Yes response and 0 for a No response to carry the statistical meaning. Since the research identifies three major computer security programs as an online capable guardianship measure, the possible range for the number of installed computer security programs is between 0 to 3.

The second observed variable also consisted of three items. The participants were presented with a series of three visual analogues consisting of a 10-month period. The participants were asked to indicate on a 10-centimeter line their responses regarding each of the three main computer security measures (firewalls, antivirus, and spyware). Their level of agreement or disagreement with each statement would identify whether they had the specific computer security program on their personal or lap top computers during the 10-month period. This 10-centimeter line, or visual analog scale, has the major advantage of being "potentially very sensitive" (DeVellis, 2003, p. 82). Thus, it would be useful for delineating the minute differences in characteristics among the participants. The terms "strongly agree" and "strongly disagree" anchor the 10-centimeter response line. Each line has range of 0 to 10, with the total possible aggregate scale range of 0 to 30 (10 x 3), with higher scores reflecting higher level of digital guardianship.

Figure 3 is an example from the survey.

Figure 3. *Digital guardian scale.*

I always had antispyware software on my computer during the last 10 months.

Strongly Disagree _____ Strongly Agree

Prior to administering the survey, potential respondents were supplied with a presurvey guideline. The presurvey guideline provided respondents with definitions of the three digital guardian measures and asked the potential respondents to examine their personal or laptop computer so that they could determine, prior to participation in the actual survey, whether they had any of the digital guardian measures already installed on their computers. The purpose of the presurvey guideline was to ensure content validity in the portion of the actual survey focusing on digital guardian measure.

In addition, it allowed the potential respondents to understand the nature of each of the digital guardian measures and assist them in identifying the brand names of those digital guardians. Asking the potential respondents in advance to identify whether such programs were installed, along with the brand name increased the accuracy of the computer security measurement, thus increasing the strength of the content validity of this project. It is of note that this presurvey guideline was not utilized in the overall data analysis of the actual survey, as its only purpose is to allow the potential respondents, prior to participation in the actual survey, to examine their personal or laptop computer so that they can determine the number, if any, of the digital guardian measures already installed on their computers.

Furthermore, a presurvey guideline was provided to the potential respondents during the class period on the class meeting day that immediately proceeds the class day when the actual survey was administered. For example, if class met on Monday, Wednesday, and Friday, and the actual survey was administered that Friday, the presurvey guideline was distributed during the Wednesday class meeting. Distributing this presurvey guideline in this fashion minimized the chances that the potential participants might forget to examine their computers prior to participating in the actual survey.

ONLINE LIFESTYLE MEASURE

Moitra (2005) assumed that computer-crime victimization can be traced from a combination of the victim's usage of the Internet and the individual behaviors within social networking places where "more victims can be targeted and in quicker succession" (p. 456).

The online target suitability was reexamined via Hindelang et al. (1978)'s theoretical perspectives. Hindelang et al. (1978) asserted that an individual lifestyle is formulated from a person's vocational and leisure activities. Online users can access the Internet to communicate with others, to search for information, to download various materials, or to shop for various products as a part of an online life. Fattach (1991) defined lifestyle as the continuous patterns "in which individuals channel their time and energy by engaging in a number activities" (p. 319). Like other crime victims, computer-crime victims also have certain personal traits that facilitate their cyber-victimization.

The present study followed two of Hindelang et al.'s (1978) propositions: Proposition 1 is that "the more time individuals spend in public places the more likely it is that they will be victimized" (p. 253). Since this proposed research focused on computer-crime victimization, the researcher set a new hypothesis as applied in cyberspace: The more time online users spend in cyberspace, the greater the chance they will be victimized. It is natural to speculate that the likelihood of being victimized in cyberspace depends on the users' online-routine activities and online lifestyles due to the level of exposure to computer criminals. Compared to people who rarely use the Internet, people who frequently use the Internet are more likely to be victimized in cyberspace. Thus, this study included an inquiry regarding how many hours the students engage in various online activities. The responses regarding these activities were measured as an online lifestyle observed variable.

Hindelang et al.'s (1978) second proposition is that "variations in lifestyle influence the convenience, desirability and ease of victimizing individuals" (p. 272). Hindelang et al. (1978) asserted that a convergence of a number of factors is required before any victimization events occur. In street crime, motivated offenders may select certain individuals whom they believe will be suitable targets of their offenses. In addition, the victims and the offenders must meet in certain places that are suitable for the commission of the offenses. This proposition reinforces this researcher's belief that routine activities theory is an expansion of lifestyle-exposure theory.

Cyberspace also provides the necessary crime-conducive places, such as social networking Web sites including computer file downloading places that provide the opportunities for computer criminals to engage in their criminal behavior. It is proposed here that computer-crime victims also tend to engage in risky online lifestyle activities in social networking Web sites in cyberspace. This strengthens the proposition that these social networking Web sites will offer greater criminal opportunities. In fact, "the crimes can be committed faster, more remotely, and possibly with less residual evidence" (Moitra, 2005, p. 456). Thus, the potential is heightened for computer criminals to victimize unwary users by surreptitiously passing spyware programs or hidden viruses into the unsuspecting user's computer system.

This research argued that social networking Web sites would be the motivated offenders' selected target areas, as they are convenient places for committing an offense, and they simultaneously attract a number of victims. In other words, online users who accept the computer criminals' offers, or visit unknown Web sites without precaution, are readily exposing themselves to computer-crime victimization. As these risky behaviors are likely to foster a high level of potential victimization from computer criminals, the proposed research placed online risky activities as the second major component that contributes to the online computer victimization, as it increases the target suitability.

This research added a third proposition to the equation. This proposition is the level of cyber-security management associated with an individual's online lifestyle. Appropriate computer security management is a crucial element of implementation to protect the online users' computer system from various computer-crime attacks. Negligence of managing up-to-date computer security programs would open up the criminal opportunities to computer criminals even if the online user had installed the three security programs on his or her personal or laptop computer.

Computer criminals generate various malevolent viruses every day, and even tight computer security systems are unable to protect against all the new virus attacks (Britz, 2004). However, updating computer security, changing passwords, and checking that the computer security is turned on before connecting to the Internet are essential to minimizing computer-crime victimization. Thus, proper computer security management substantially impacts on the crime victimization. In other words, the efficient management of up-to-date computer securities would minimize the level of computer criminal target suitability.

Thus, the most effective protection against computer-crime victimization, aside from never going on the Internet, is one that applies the requisite three observed variables. Therefore, this study hypothesized that online users who have risky online behaviors, who lack adequate cyber-security management, and who engage in extensive online hours are more likely to be victimized.

As shown in Figure 4, online lifestyle consists of three observed variables from three different online lifestyle perspectives. For the first measure of online lifestyle, nine survey items were designed to rate the respondents' vocational and leisure activities on the Internet. Examples of the nine items are "I frequently checked my e-mail during the last 10 months," "I frequently spent time shopping on the Internet during the last 10 months," "I frequently spent time on the Internet to entertain myself during the last 10 months," and "I frequently spent time on the Internet when I was bored during the last 10 months."

Respondents were asked to indicate on a 10-centimeter response line their level of agreement or disagreement with each statement. This 10-centimeter line, or visual analog scale, has the major advantage of being "potentially very sensitive" (DeVellis, 2003). Thus, it would be useful for delineating the minute differences in characteristics among the participants. The terms strongly agree and strongly disagree anchor the 10-centimeter response line. The scale's possible aggregate range is 0 to 90, with higher scores reflecting higher online vocational and leisure activities.

Figure 4. *Online lifestyle measure.*

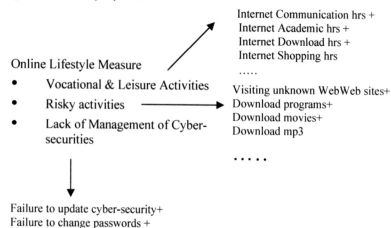

Online Lifestyle Measure

- Vocational & Leisure Activities
- Risky activities
- Lack of Management of Cyber-securities

Internet Communication hrs +
Internet Academic hrs +
Internet Download hrs +
Internet Shopping hrs
.....

Visiting unknown WebWeb sites+
Download programs+
Download movies+
Download mp3
.....

Failure to update cyber-security+
Failure to change passwords +
Go online w/o first ensuring that cyber-security measures are operational
.....

The second part of the questionnaire contains nine survey items that were designed to rate the respondents' online risky activities. Examples of the nine items are, "I frequently visited Web sites that were new to me during the last 10 months," "I frequently downloaded free games that interested me from any Web sites during the last 10 months," "I frequently opened any attachment in e-mails that I received during the last 10 months," and "I frequently opened any file or attachment I received through my instant messenger during the last 10 months." Respondents were asked to indicate on a 10-centimeter response line their level of agreement or disagreement with each statement. The terms strongly agree and strongly disagree anchor the response line. The scale's possible aggregate range is 0 to 90, with the higher scores reflecting higher online risky activities.

The third part of the questionnaire contains five survey items that were designed to rate the computer security management measure. Examples of the five items are, "I frequently changed passwords for my e-mail accounts during the last 10 months," "I frequently updated my computer security software during the last 10 months," "I frequently checked to make sure my computer security software was on before I used the Internet during the last 10 months," and "I used different passwords and user IDs for each of my Internet accounts during the last 10 months." Respondents were asked to indicate on a 10-centimeter response line their level of agreement or disagreement with each statement. The terms strongly agree and strongly disagree anchor the response line. In order to measure the lack of computer security management, the obtained values from the respondents will be reverse coded in the statistical analysis process. Thus, the scale's possible aggregate range is 0 to 50, with the higher scores reflecting lower levels of computer security management.

COMPUTER-CRIME VICTIMIZATION MEASURE

Moitra (2005) asserts that the nature of the online environment subjects the Internet users to experience a proportionally higher level of victimization than they would experience from traditional crimes. The research has adapted the existing scales from 2004 Australian Computer Crime and Security Survey, and this research identifies the overall endogenous variable "computer-crime victimization" as containing three distinct observed variables: total frequency of victimization, total number of hours lost, and total monetary loss. Examples of the three items are, "In the last 10 months, how many times did you have computer virus infection incidents," "In the last 10 months, approximately how many hours were spent fixing your computer due to the virus infections?, and "In the last 10 months, approximately how much money did you spend fixing your computer due to computer virus infections?" Thus, each of these observed variables, once measured, should reveal a clear picture of the individual's repeat victimization, the time consumption, and the individual economic loss.

CONVERGENCE OF TWO LATENT VARIABLES MEASURE

The hypotheses espoused earlier in this study, combined with the digital-capable guardian's measures and online lifestyle measures, should provide an accurate estimate of the computer-crime victimization experienced by the survey participants. In sum, the proposed Computer-Crime Victimization Model assumed that computer-crime victims are more susceptible to personal computer victimization compared to other online users who use the Internet less, who frequently have the necessary computer security programs installed on their computers, who properly manage, including up-dating, the installed computer security programs, and who avoid risky online behaviors. The researcher expected to observe an interaction effect by examining the convergence of the online lifestyles and the digital-capable guardianships that directly impact on victimization. Furthermore, the new model empowers both the lifestyle-exposure theory and routine activities theory by combining details on online target suitability and target hardening through the digital-capable guardianship.

Figure 5 depicts the complete Computer-Crime Victimization Model based on application of the tenets from each of the two previously discussed theories. The model indicates that the digital guardian latent variable has a direct impact on computer-crime victimization. The online lifestyle latent variable also directly influences the level of computer-crime victimization. It is of note that this computer-crime victimization model has never been previously proposed or assessed in criminology literature. Thus, this model conveys the foundation of a computer-crime individual victimization study that should identify patterns of computer-crime victimization.

Figure 5. *Hybrid model.*

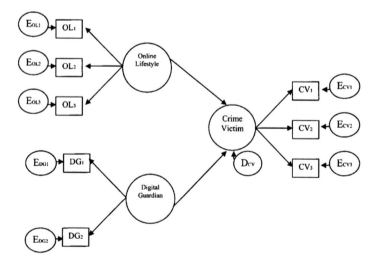

The measurement model represents the relationship between crime victimization and the two exogenous latent variables, digital guardian and online lifestyle. In Figure 6, there is a bidirectional arrow that indicates unmeasured relationships. The bidirectional arrow indicates the unmeasured covariance between the digital guardianship and the online lifestyle. As evidenced by the bidirectional arrow there is no revealed, or defined, causal direction.

Figure 6. *Measurement model.*

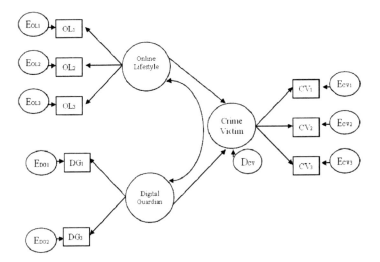

The diagram also indicates that scores on the survey items are caused by two correlated factors, along with the variance that is unique to each item. In order to set the scale of measurement for the latent factors and residuals, the paths' coefficients have fixed values set to a value of one. Setting variances of the factors to value of one provides a scale for the factor and implicit standardized solutions.

The measurement model was tested by a confirmatory factor analysis (CFA) in order to reveal whether the latent variables are precisely reflected in the observed variables. The researcher expected to gain a pattern of results that reveal that each variable loads highly onto one factor per each latent variable via the performance of confirmatory factor analysis. If the measurement model satisfies the pattern of results, the proposed structural model will be successfully tested. If the measurement model does not satisfy the pattern of results, the observed variables should be reexamined to meet the requirement for the assessment of the structural model.

SEM was used to assess the proposed computer-crime victimization model. SEM will delineate relationships between the observed variables and the latent variables via "the structural parameters defined by a hypothesized underlying model" (Kaplan, 1995,p.1).

As a powerful statistical method, the significant function of flexibility controlling nonnormal distributions, missing data, and multilevel data in SEM enables one to incorporate a complex measurement model into a more general statistical model. In addition, SEM operates factor analysis and path analysis as the two main statistical methodological functions that are crucial to test the central propositions in the model

CHAPTER 4

SEM Assessment: Cyber-Routine Activities Theoretical Model

The main premise of two traditional victimization theories, routine activities theory (Cohen & Felson, 1979) and lifestyle-exposure theory (Hindelang, Gottfredson, & Garofalo, 1978) have applied to link primary causations of computer-crime victimization. From the routine activities theoretical perspective, one of three tenets, capable guardian, was identified as a main causal factor that contributes to computer-crime victimization, because this project assumes that the most feasible method of preventing computer-crime victimization is a target-hardening strategy by equipping adequate computer security software, referred to as digital guardians in this project. Since the operation of formal social control agents in cyberspace is limited, the research posits that estimating the level of equipping adequate computer security in the computer system determines the degree of computer-crime victimization. From the lifestyle-exposure theoretical perspective, one of the research interests is to measure the level of target suitability by examining individual online lifestyle that potentially contributes to computer-crime victimization. The research assumes that the levels of online vocational and leisure activities, and the degree of online risk-taking behaviors would produce greater or lesser opportunities for computer-crime victimization.

SAMPLE

In the first phase of the analysis, a comparison was made between the sample and the population. For the class selection, among 579 classes (freshmen level: 364 classes, sophomore level: 149 classes, upperclassmen level: 66 classes), 12 classes based on class level were randomly selected, using SPSS 14 (SPSS, 2006). The purpose of randomly selecting 12 classes was to fulfill the requirement of gaining minimum of 10 classes for ensuring a sufficient sample size. However, a total of 25% (3 out of 12 selected classes) of the course instructors refused to allow the researcher to administer the survey because of time constraints. This was mainly due to the fact that the survey was administered at the end of semester (prior to the final exam week). A total of 345 respondents took part in the study, and 204 respondents fully completed the survey. Of the original 345 surveys, 141 surveys were not used. Twenty-five were turned in incomplete, and 116 students (about 33% of the sample population based on a total of 345) did not participate in this study because they did not own their own desktop or laptop computer. Hence, a useable sample of 204 surveys was analyzed for this project.

Table 2 below presents four specific demographic items (age, gender, race, and class) that indicate the comparison between the population and sample. Although the sample differs from the population in the area of class standing, the results demonstrate that the sample characteristic is similar to the population for age and gender. In terms of race category, the sample provides a good estimate of representation. Although there is a 5.5 % greater percentage of Caucasian students compared to the population, the percent of African American students in the sample is identical to the population and all other race categories in the sample are similar to the population. The sample provides a difference from the population for class standing in freshman and upperclassmen. While being underrepresented with the upperclassmen sample and overrepresented with freshman sample, the sophomore sample represents the population. This result can be explained by the three upperclassmen classes for which the professor denied access by the researcher. It is unlikely that the differences found will substantially impact the validity of the results because class standing differences should not be considered as a main factor that contributes to computer-crime victimization.

Even though this sample cannot be fully considered as representative of the population on the basis of the demographic variables on which the sample and population were compared, the composition of the sample is not a major concern in this study.

Table 2
Comparison of Sample and Population on Available Demographic Characteristics

Demographic characteristic		A undergraduate student population $(N = 12,047)^*$	Study sample $(N = 204)$
Age			
	Mean age	20	20.41
Gender			
	Female	55.3% ($n = 6,656$)	54.9% ($n = 112$)
	Male	44.7% ($n = 5,391$)	45.1% ($n = 92$)
Race			
	African American	7.4% ($n = 879$)	7.4% ($n = 15$)
	Asian	.9% ($n = 104$)	2% ($n = 4$)
	Caucasian	78.8% ($n = 9,505$)	84.3% ($n = 172$)
	Hispanic	1.1% ($n = 137$)	2% ($n = 4$)
	Native American	.2% ($n = 29$)	0% ($n = 0$)
	Other	11.6% ($n = 1393$)	4.4% ($n = 9$)
Class			
	Freshman	34% ($n = 4,086$)	40.7% ($n = 83$)
	Sophomore	22% ($n = 2,638$)	23% ($n = 47$)
	Upperclassmen	44% ($n = 5,323$)	36.3% ($n = 74$)

* *Note.* Source: 2006 Trendbook and State System Factbook

PROPERTIES OF MEASURES

As discussed in the methods section of this book, new observed variables were developed for each of the primary latent variables. The digital guardian latent variable consisted of two observed variables, and each online lifestyle and computer-crime victimization latent variables consist of three observed variables. The main importance of this research is whether each of the digital guardian and the online lifestyle latent variable has a direct impact on computer-crime victimization. Each section addresses the relationship among individuals' level of the digital-capable guardianship, online lifestyle, and computer-crime victimization. In addition, each section individually presents the assessment of qualities of measures through testing reliability and item-total correlation along with descriptive statistics for each of the observed variables. In order to assess whether observed variables are unidimensional, results of a Scree test are presented for each scale.

Two steps that are used to measure the quality of these scales are as follows:

Step 1: The reliability and validity of each of the constructs was assessed. The internal consistency via Cronbach's alpha represents the amount of variance in scale score among the items. DeVellis's (2003) reliability standards for research scales are as follows: "below an alpha coefficient of .60, unacceptable; an alpha coefficient between .60 and .65, undesirable; an alpha coefficient between .65 and .70, minimally acceptable; between .70 and .80, respectable; between .80 and .90, very good; much above, one should consider shortening the scale" (pp. 95-96). Item-total correlations were also assessed to determine whether items are considered as a set of highly intercorrelated items. An item-total correlation value of .30 or above indicated appropriate shared variance among the items.

In addition, skewness was assessed to examine how much scores cluster on one side of a distribution or the other. The general guideline of the skewness coefficient was below the absolute value of 3.0 for the analysis of SEM that conveys an optimal operation (Giever, 1995; Higgins, 2001). Furthermore, kurtosis measured the peakedness of a distribution, including clustered scores around a central point based on their standard deviation. A kurtosis coefficient below the absolute value of 10 indicated normally distributed data that allows an optimal SEM analysis (Giever, 1995; Higgins, 2001).

Step 2: As a data reduction technique, the Cattell Scree test was used to transform from a set of variables into smaller sets of variables. As discussed in the methods section, based on the preestablished victimization model, a confirmatory factor analysis (CFA) was utilized to determine whether the loadings of measured variables represent each latent variable in the model. In this study, a varimax rotation was used to identify factor loadings in each scale items with a single observed variable through an orthogonal rotation for ensuring the quality of magnitude of factor loading. Since each of observed variables consist of multiple items, it is important to verify whether each set of observed variables are constructed as unimensionality.

If certain item(s) did not have in common with other items, the item was removed; then, reliability and validity were reassessed. Once individual items were confirmed as a unitary construct of each observed variable via CFA, a confirmatory factor analysis was reassessed to ensure whether each of set of observed variables was considered as each of unidimensional latent variables. If the measurement model did not satisfy the pattern of results, the observed variables were reexamined to meet the requirement for the assessment of the structural model.

Digital Guardian

In terms of the digital-capable guardianship, this project previously identified the three most common digital-capable guardians available to online users: antivirus program, antispyware program, and firewalls program. Each of digital guardians has its own distinctive function to protect computer system from computer criminals. First digital guardian, an antivirus program, mainly monitors whether computer viruses have gained an access through digital files, software, or hardware, and if the antivirus computer software finds a virus, the software attempts to delete or isolate it to prevent a threat to the computer system (Moore, 2005). The second digital guardian is a firewall program that is mainly designed to prevent computer criminals from accessing the computer system over the online network; however, unlike the antivirus software, firewalls do not detect or eliminate viruses (Casey, 2000). The last digital guardian, antispyware program, is mainly designed to prevent spyware from being installed in the computer system (Casey, 2000). Once spyware is being installed, it intercepts users' valuable digital information such as passwords or credit card numbers as a user enters them into a Web form or other applications (Ramsastry, 2004, p. 13).

The researcher posits that the level of capable digital guardianship, in the form of installed computer security systems, will differentiate the level of computer-crime victimization. Thus, the number of installed security programs on a computer and the duration of equipping the installed security programs was measured in order to estimate the level of digital-capable guardianship.

The first observed variable consisted of three items that asked the respondents to state what types of computer security they had in their own computer prior to participation in the survey. The three items were based on dichotomous structure, which was identified 0 as absence of security and 1 as presence of security. The possible range for the number of installed computer security programs was between 0 to 3. The value 0 refers to absence of computer security and 3 means that computer users installed antivirus, antisoftware, and firewall software in their own computer. The mean of the number of computer security score for this sample was 2.6, with a standard deviation of .73, a skewness of -1.96, and a kurtosis of 3.37.

The internal consistency coefficient of .62 appearing in Table 3 indicates undesirable range of Cronbach's alpha based on DeVellis's (2003) reliability standards. However, the item-total correlations (Item 1 = .40, Item 2 = .43, and Item 3 = .44) were respectable, with all three items above the acceptable levels of item total correlations of .30.

The second observed variable also consisted of three items with a series of three visual analogues by asking the participants to indicate on a 10-centimeter line their responses regarding each of the three main computer security measures (antivirus, antisypware, and firewalls). Their level of agreement with each statement was identified by asking whether they had the specific computer security program on their personal or lap top computers during the 10-month period. Each line had a range of 0 to 10, with the total possible range for this capable guardian scale between 0 and 30. The mean of the duration of having computer security score for this sample was 22.3, with a standard deviation of 7.65, a skewness of -.99, and a kurtosis of .25.

The data indicate that this digital guardian scale had an adequate alpha coefficient of .70 that was sufficient for research purposes. All three scale items (Item 1 = .50, Item 2 = .52, and Item 3 = .55) performed well and sufficiently met the acceptable levels of item-total correlation of .30 (see Table 4).

An assessment of the psychometric properties of digital guardianship indicates that each of the scales has satisfactory skewness and kurtosis levels. The skewness for each of the scales was well below the suggested level of the absolute value of 3.0. In addition, the scales were not overly peaked and the kurtosis levels were also well below the absolute value of 10.0. Even though the shapes of histograms suggested that the scales have not fully met the appropriate levels of normality, the scales have met the appropriate levels of skewness and kurtosis for SEM analysis, (see Figures 7 and 8). In addition, the scales had adequate item-total correlations and the internal consistency coefficient for research purposes.

Table 3

Item-Total Correlations for Digital Guardian (Number of Security): Three Items

Item		Item total correlation	Cronbach's alpha if item deleted
1.	Did you have antivirus software on your computer during the last 10 months?	.40	.55
2.	Did you have antispyware software on your computer during the last 10 months?	.43	.42
3.	Did you have firewall software on your computer during the last 10 months?	.44	.41

Cronbach's Alpha = .62

Table 4

Item-Total Correlations for Digital Guardian (Duration of Having Security): Three Items

Item	Item total correlation	Cronbach's alpha if item deleted
1. I always had antivirus software on my computer during the last 10 months.	.50	.64
2. I always had antispyware software on my computer during the last 10 months.	.52	.60
3. I always had firewall software on my computer during the last 10 months.	.55	.56

Cronbach's Alpha = .70

    An assessment of the unidimensionality of the measures of the constructs for each of observed variables can be measured by utilizing factor analysis with the application of the Cattell Scree test (Giever, 1995: Loehlin, 1992). It is important to be aware of utilizing dichotomous variables with factor analysis (Kim & Mueller, 1978). However, Giever (1995) asserted that if the purpose of using the method is to identify for a clustering pattern, the use of factor analysis is valid. Thus, the first observed variable based on dichotomous structure is permissible to use in a factor analysis. The logic of the Scree test is to examine the most significant break in eigenvalues based on the principal components factor analysis for the digital guardian scale (Giever, 1995).

    The eigenvalues for the principal components analysis of each of observed digital guardian are shown in Tables 5 and 6. The unidimensionality of the scales is assessed utilizing Cattell's Scree test with principal components factor analysis using a varimax rotation. Tables 5 and 6 present the eigenvalues from the principal components factor analysis for each scale. The results indicate that there is one very clear factor for each observed variable, with eigenvalues of 1.69 and 1.88, respectively. Upon further examination, after the first factor, each of factors was not very different from the other factors that have eigenvalues below 1. This can be seen in the Scree plot, which shows that the eigenvalues level off after the first factor. The rotated loadings in the each of the"Component Matrix" for Factor 1 are all positive and relatively large (see Tables 7 and 8). This indicates that Factor 1 is essentially the total of the responses over all three items.

Table 5
Principal Components Analysis (Varimax Rotation) of Digital Guardian: Number of Security

Factor	Eigenvalue
1	1.69
2	.68
3	.63

Figure 7. *Scree plot for digital guardian items: Number of security.*

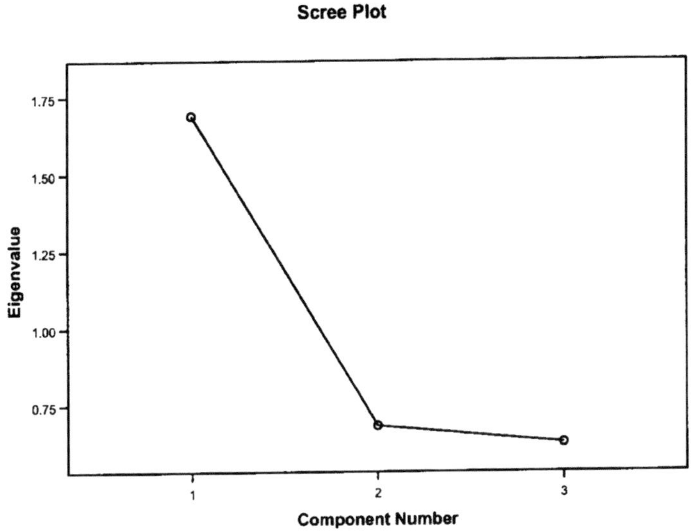

Scree Plot

Table 6
*Principal Components Analysis (Varimax Rotation) of Digital
Guardian: Duration of Having Installed Security*

Factor	Eigenvalue
1	1.88
2	.59
3	.52

Figure 8. *Scree plot for digital guardian items: Duration of having
installed security.*

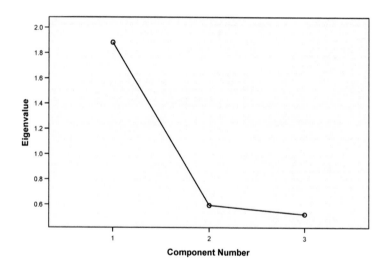

Table 7
Component Matrix (Varimax Rotation) of Digital Guardian

	Component
Did you have Antivirus?	.729
Did you have Antispyware?	.761
Did you have Firewall?	.761

Extraction Method: Principal Component Analysis.

Table 8

Component Matrix (Varimax Rotation) of Digital Guardian

	Component
Antivirus on my computer	.776
Antispyware on my computer	.788
Firewall on my computer	.812

Extraction Method: Principal Component Analysis.

CFA on Digital-Capable Guardianship

After gaining confirmation of the unidimensionality for each of observed variables via confirmatory factor analysis, the research reassessed the unidimensionality. The purpose of utilizing CFA here is to determine whether two observed digital guardian variables truly become one single digital guardian latent variable. In fact, having certain number of computer security components in an online user's computer does not fully reflect the duration of equipping the security programs. Thus, it is essential to examine whether both observed variables can be represented as one digital guardian measure through CFA.

Since the results indicate that each of observed variables consists of unidimensional structure, the sum of the combination of individual item scores should be represented as each of the observed variables. After establishing each of three-item cumulative scales based on each of observed variables, factor analysis was reapplied.

The eigenvalues for the principal components analysis of digital guardian are given in Table 9. The assessment of the eigenvalues above and the Scree plot presented in Figure 9 illustrates that there is a clear indication of a single latent factor which is indicative of a unidimensional trait. In addition, the elements of "Component Matrix" for Factor 1 are all positive and significantly large (see Table 10).

An inspection of the Scree plot also provides support that the digital guardian scale consists of a unitary construct. Thus, the results confirm that a single digital guardian latent variable consists of computer security and duration of having the installed computer security during the 10-month period. This finding also suggests that it is important to take the number of computer security components and duration of equipping the computer security in an online user's computer into consideration for producing adequate digital guardian measure. In sum, the digital guardian scales have met the basic measurement criteria for SEM. The scales have acceptable reliability, acceptable item-total correlations, acceptable skewness and kurtosis levels, and the observed variables were unidimensional.

Table 9
Principal Components Analysis (Varimax Rotation) of Digital Guardian

Factor	Eigenvalue
1	1.79
2	.22

Figure 9. *Scree plot for digital guardian items.*

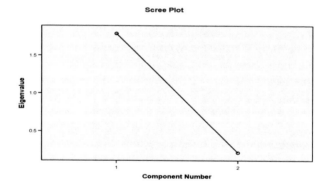

Table 10
Component Matrix (Varimax Rotation) of Digital Guardian

	Component
Number of computer security	.945
Duration: Having the installed computer security	.945

Extraction Method: Principal Component Analysis.

Online Lifestyle

Britz (2004) asserted that even tight computer security systems do not fully protect against all the new virus attacks since computer criminals generate various malevolent viruses on a daily basis. The research found that different online vocational and leisure activities on the Internet offer different levels of risk of victimization. The researcher posited that users' online lifestyle is also a substantial factor to minimize the computer-crime victimization. Individual online lifestyle is measured by three distinct observed variables. The first observed variable examines online users' vocational and leisure activities by estimating time spent in cyberspace. It was posited that the more time online users spend in cyberspace, the greater the chance they will be victimized. The second observed variable was to measure variations in risky online lifestyle that differentiate the level of computer-crime victimization. The research placed online risky activities as a crucial component that contributes to online computer-crime victimization. The level of cyber-security management scales were constructed as the third observed variable that may protect the online users' computer system from computer-crime attack. The research posits that the efficient management of up-to-date computer security minimizes the level of computer criminal target suitability. Thus, online lifestyle factor was the basis of measuring presented three observed variables.

As stated above, the online lifestyle latent variable consists of three different observed variables: (a) vocational and leisure activities on the Internet, (b) online risky activities, and (c) computer security management. In order to estimate accurate measures for each of the observed variable, the psychometric properties (mean, standard deviation, skewness, kurtosis, item-total correlations, and alpha coefficient) for each observed variable were individually examined prior to estimating the unidmensionality of the online lifestyle scales as a single latent variable.

For the first measure of online lifestyle, nine survey items that make up the vocational and leisure activities scale, along with their item-total correlations, are shown in Table 11 below. As with the vocational and leisure activities scale, respondents were asked to indicate on a 10-centimeter response line their level of agreement or disagreement with each statement. The items were anchored by strongly agree at the lower limit and strongly disagree at the upper limit.

Table 11

Item-Total Correlations for Vocational and Leisure Activities: Nine Items

Item		Item total correlation	Cronbach's alpha if item deleted
1.	I frequently checked my e-mail during the last 10 months.	.32	.61
2.	I frequently used an instant messenger (e.g., MSN, AOL, etc.) to communicate with people during the last 10 months.	.33	.60
3.	I frequently spent time downloading materials from the Internet during the last 10 months.	.31	.60
4.	I frequently spent time shopping on the Internet during the last 10 months.	.21	.62
5.	I frequently spent time on the Internet to entertain myself during the last 10 months.	.52	.55
6.	I frequently spent time on the Internet for study purpose during the last 10 months.	.03	.66
7.	I frequently viewed or watched news on the Internet during the last 10 months.	.35	.60
8.	I frequently sent e-mails to people during the last 10 months	.29	.61
9.	I frequently spent time on the Internet when I was bored during the last 10 months.	.52	.56

Cronbach's Alpha = .63

Table 12
Item-Total Correlations for Vocational and Leisure Activities: Five Items

Item		Item total correlation	Cronbach's alpha if item deleted
1.	I frequently checked my e-mail during the last 10 months.	.33	.64
2.	I frequently used an instant messenger (e.g., MSN, AOL, etc.) to communicate with people during the last 10 months.	.37	.62
3.	I frequently spent time downloading materials from the Internet during the last 10 months.	.34	.63
4.	I frequently spent time shopping on the Internet during the last 10 months.	.21	.66
5.	I frequently spent time on the Internet to entertain myself during the last 10 months.	.55	.57
6.	I frequently viewed or watched news on the Internet during the last 10 months.	.30	.64
7.	I frequently sent e-mails to people during the last 10 months	.26	.64
8.	I frequently spent time on the Internet when I was bored during the last 10 months.	.54	.58

Cronbach's Alpha = .66

The scale's possible aggregate range is 0 to 90 with higher scores reflecting higher online vocational and leisure activities. The Cronbach's alpha was .63, which is below what is considered adequate for a scale to be used for the purposes. These findings suggest that some of the items do not share much variance in common, so removing the variables, which do not represent the common underlying construct of vocational and leisure activities, should increase the validity of the vocational and leisure activities scales.

The assessment of Cronbach's alpha for this category identified one item that substantially does not represent the common underlying construct of vocational and leisure activities. Reliability test suggest that this item (B6: I frequently spent time on the Internet for study purposes during the last 10 months) contributed to produce lower reliability. The item total correlation of .03 clearly indicates that this item significantly reduces alpha. Thus, one item out of the total nine items was excluded from the proposed model.

The psychometric properties for the rest of eight items appear in Table 12. After removing the worst item, which contributed to lower reliability, the data indicate that the vocational and leisure activities scale has an adequate alpha coefficient of .66 that is more acceptable for research purposes. Even though Item 4 and 7 (Item 4 = .21 and Item 7 = .26) had an item-total correlation below the acceptable level of .30, most scale items (Item 1 = .33, Item 2 = .37, Item 3 = .34, Item 5 = .55, Item 6 = .30, and Item 8 = .54) performed well and sufficiently met the acceptable levels of item-total correlation of .30. This suggests that these eight items are better measures of vocational and leisure activities and should remain part of the vocational and leisure activities scale for research purposes.

Since eight items are viable in the category of vocational and leisure activities, the scale's possible aggregate range is 0 to 80. The mean vocational and leisure activities score for this sample is 53.62, with a standard deviation of 11.22. The scale based on five items had satisfactory skewness and kurtosis levels. A skewness of -.60 was well below the suggested level of the absolute value of 3.0. In addition, a kurtosis of 1.01 revealed that the scales are not overly peaked and well below the absolute value of 10.0. Thus, the results from skewness and kurtosis indicated that the scales have met the appropriate levels of normality for SEM analysis (See Figure 10).

The unidimensionality of the scales is assessed utilizing Cattell's Scree test with principal components factor analysis using varimax rotation (see Figure 10). Table 13 presents the eigenvalues from the principal components factor analysis for the scale reflecting the eight survey items.

The results indicated that there are three factors, with an eigenvalue of 2.58, 1.32, and 1.16, respectively. Unfortunately, the results did not convey a clear unitary construct of vocational and leisure activities based on Kaiser's rule in factor analysis. Kaiser's rule only accounts factors, which obtain number of eigenvalues of greater than 1 (Darlington, 2008, p. 81).

In fact, many factor analysts argue that factor analysis can be a subjective statistical method when a researcher wants to report only interpretable factor by conveniently controlling undesirable items (Darlington, 2008, p. 13). This research focused on developing a valid and reliable construct rather than removing items, which may hinder a unitary construct. In the results, Factor 1 accounts for over 32% of the variance, which presents as the most substantial indicative factor. In contrast to Factor 1, eigenvalue of Factor 2 and 3 are slightly greater than 1, and they were not very different from the other factors that have eigenvalues below 1.

This can be seen in the Scree plot, which shows a clear "elbow" of the eigenvalues level off after the first factor. In addition, "Component Matrix" (see Table 14) for the first factor was clearly marked by high loadings on the most items (B1 = .540, B2 = .619, B3 = .451, B5 = .775, B6 = .448, B7 = .457, and B8 = .799) except for one item (B4 = .238). Since Scree test examines a significant break where the plot immediately levels out, this research validated the scale items as a unitary construct.

Even though the results did not convey an optimal unitary construct based on the Kaiser's rule, the findings suggested that Factor 1 is primarily the total of the responses over all eight items. In other words, the eight items are regarded as one online vocational and leisure activities factor in the research.

The vocational and leisure activities scales have met the basic measurement criteria for SEM. The scales have acceptable reliability, acceptable item-total correlations, acceptable skewness and kurtosis levels, and the scale items are treated as an approximate unidimensional construct.

Table 13
Principal Components Analysis (Varimax Rotation) of Vocational and Leisure Activities

Factor	Eigenvalue
1	2.58
2	1.32
3	1.16
4	.92
5	.65
6	.57
7	.50
8	.31

Figure 10. *Scree plot for vocational and leisure items.*

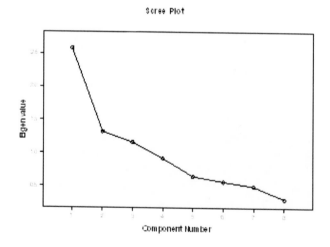

Table 14
Component Matrix of Vocational and Leisure Activities: Eight items

	Component		
	1	2	3
E-mail	.540	-.567	.292
Instant Messenger	.619	-.035	-.341
Downloading Materials	.451	.593	.028
Online Shopping	.238	.580	.609
Entertainment	.775	.120	-.336
News	.448	.286	.241
Sent E-mail	.457	-.450	.596
Spent time on the Internet When I was bored	.799	-.117	-.266

Extraction Method: Principal Component Analysis.

For the second measure of online lifestyle, nine survey items that are designed to rate the respondents' online risky activities. Like other online lifestyle scale, respondents were asked to indicate on a 10-centimeter response line their level of agreement or disagreement with each statement. The terms "strongly agree" and "strongly disagree" anchor the response line. Table 15 presents the online risky activities scale, along with their item-total correlations.

The item-total correlations appearing in Table 15 are respectable, with only one falling below .30. The internal consistency coefficient of .70 is adequate reliability for research purposes (see Table 15). Since the assessment indicates that the item number 2 (I frequently visited social networking Web sites such as myspace.com during the last 10 months) in the online risky activities has a low item total correlation of .22 that contributes to a low level of reliability, the item was removed from the research. Hence, the total of eight items was reassessed as the online risky activities after removing the first item. The reassessed reliability test shows that dropping the item number 2 increased alpha (see Table 15-1).

Table 15

Item-Total Correlations for Vocational and Leisure Activities: Nine Items

Item		Item total correlation	Cronbach's alpha if item deleted
1	I frequently visited Web sites that were new to me during the last 10 months.	.34	.69
2	I frequently visited social networking Web sites such as my space.com during the last 10 months.	.22	.71
3	I frequently downloaded free games from any Web site during the last 10 months.	.41	.68
4	I frequently downloaded free music that interested me from any Web site during the last 10 months.	.37	.69
5	I frequently downloaded free movies that interested me from any Web site during the last 10 months.	.40	.69
6	I frequently opened any attachment in the e-mails that I received during the last 10 months.	.38	.66
7	I frequently clicked on any Web-links in the e-mails that I received during the last 10 months.	.50	.66
8	I frequently opened any file or attachment I received through my instant messenger during the last 10 months.	.52	.66
9	I frequently clicked on a pop-up message that interested me during the last 10 months.	.40	.69

Cronbach's Alpha = .70

Table 15-1
Item-Total Correlations for Vocational and Leisure Activities: Eight Items

Item		Item total correlation	Cronbach's alpha if item deleted
1	I frequently visited Web sites that were new to me during the last 10 months.	.33	.70
2	I frequently downloaded free games from any Web site during the last 10 months.	.42	.68
3	I frequently downloaded free music that interested me from any Web site during the last 10 months.	.35	.70
4	I frequently downloaded free movies that interested me from any Web site during the last 10 months.	.40	.69
5	I frequently opened any attachment in the e-mails that I received during the last 10 months.	.39	.69
6	I frequently clicked on any Web-links in the e-mails that I received during the last 10 months.	.50	.66
7	I frequently opened any file or attachment I received through my instant messenger during the last 10 months.	.51	.66
8	I frequently clicked on a pop-up message that interested me during the last 10 months.	.42	.70

Cronbach's Alpha = .71

Interestingly, the assessment of factor analysis for this category found that there were two subcategories within online risky activities. The component plot visually inspected two distinctive clusters of the items (see Figure 11). The first subcategory of online risky activities was differentiated with one set of four items as "online risky leisure activities," and the second subcategory was distinguished with one set of four items as "online risky vocational activities."

After reorganizing the variables reflecting two subcategories of online risky activities, the data indicated that "risky leisure activities scale" and "risky vocational activities scale" have Cronbach's alpha coefficients of .73 and .80, respectively, that are acceptable for research (see Tables 18 and 19). In the first subcategory of online risky activities, risky leisure activities, all three scale items (Item 1 = .31, Item 2 = .69, Item 3 = .66 and Item 4 = .67) performed well and adequately met the acceptable levels of item-total correlation of .30 (see Table 16). In the second subcategory of online risky activities, risky vocational activities, all four scale items (Item 1 = .72, Item 2 = .77, Item 3 = .63, and Item 4 = .41) also performed well and sufficiently met the adequate levels of item total correlation (see Table 17). Thus, for research purposes, the both scales had adequate item-total correlations.

Since only four items are viable in the first category of online risky activities ("Risky Leisure Activities"), the scale's possible aggregate range becomes 0 to 40. The mean of the first risky activities score for this sample is 16.02, with standard deviation of 8.93, a skewness of .463, and a kurtosis of -.441. The second category of online risky activities ("Risky Vocational Activities") consisted of four items, so the scale's possible aggregate range is 0 to 40. The mean of the second risky activities score for this sample was 13.21, with standard deviation of 8.89, a skewness of .372, and kurtosis of -.782.

Each of the scales in both online risky activities categories had satisfactory skewness and kurtosis levels. The skewness for each of the scales was well below the suggested level of the absolute value of 3.0. In addition, the scales were not overly peaked based on the reported kurtosis levels that are well below the absolute value of 10.0. Although the results from histograms indicate that the category of "risky vocational activities" is closer to an approximate normality than the category of "risky leisure activities," both categories have met the appropriate levels of skewness and kurtosis for SEM analysis.

Table 16
Item-Total Correlations for Risky Leisure Activities: Four Items

Item		Item total correlation
1: B10	I frequently visited Web sites that were new to me during the last 10 months.	.31
2: B12	I frequently downloaded free games from any Web site during the last 10 months.	.69
3: B13	I frequently downloaded free music that interested me from any Web site during the last 10 months.	.66
4: B14	I frequently downloaded free movies that interested me from any Web site during the last 10 months.	.67

Cronbach's Alpha = .73

Table 17
Item-Total Correlations for Risky Vocational Activities: Four Items

Item		Item total correlation
1: B15	I frequently opened any attachment in the e-mails that I received during the last 10 months.	.72
2: B16	I frequently clicked on any Web-links in the e-mails that I received during the last 10 months.	.77
3: B17	I frequently opened any file or attachment I received through my instant messenger during the last 10 months.	.63
4: B18	I frequently clicked on a pop-up message that interested me during the last 10 months.	.41

Cronbach's Alpha = .80

Figure 11. *Component plot for risky leisure activities and risky vocational activities.*

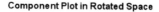

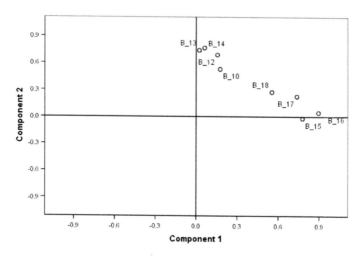

The unidimensionality of the scales was assessed utilizing Cattell's Scree test with principal components factor analysis using varimax rotation in both categories (see Figure 12 and 13). Tables 19 and 20 present the eigenvalues from the principal components factor analysis for each scale.

The results showed that exhibited one clear factor with eigenvalue of 1.96 in the first subcategory of risky leisure activities items. Similarly, the second category of risky vocational activities items also indicated one very clear factor with eigenvalue of 2.32.

In both subcategories of online risky activities, after the first factor, each of factors was not significantly different from the other factors that have eigenvalues below 1. The Scree plot also clearly verified the "elbow," which the eigenvalues level off after the first factor in each of categories. In addition, each "Component Matrix" in both categories indicates that Factor 1 contains all positive and relatively large values (see Table 20 and 21). The results supported that each of Factor 1 is essentially the total of the responses over all listed items. In other words, four items of the first subcategory and four items of the second category are respectively represented as one "risky leisure activities factor" and one "risky vocational activities factor."

Both online risky activities categories have met the basic measurement criteria for SEM. The scales in both subcategories contained acceptable reliability, acceptable item-total correlations, acceptable skewness and kurtosis levels, and observed variables have confirmed with a unidimensionality. Therefore, the researcher took into consideration both subcategories of online risky activities as two distinct observed variables in the measurement model based on the assessment of the psychometric properties by including two observed variables into the model.

Table 18
Principal Components Analysis (Varimax Rotation) of Risky Leisure Activities

Factor	Eigenvalue
1	1.96
2	.91
3	.61
4	.52

Figure 12. *Scree plot for risky leisure activities items.*

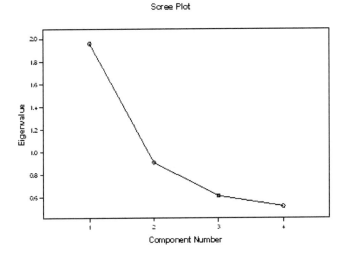

Scree Plot

Component Number

Table 19
Principal Components Analysis (Varimax Rotation) of Risky
Vocational Activities

Factor	Eigenvalue
1	2.32
2	.84
3	.55
4	.30

Figure 13. *Scree plots for risky vocational activities items.*

Scree Plot

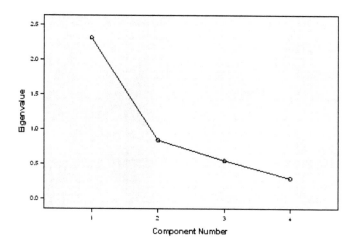

Table 20
Component Matrix (Varimax Rotation) of Risky Leisure Activities

	Component
New Web sites	.59
Free games	.72
Free music	.72
Free movie	.75

Extraction Method: Principal Component Analysis

Table 21
Component Matrix (Varimax Rotation) of Risky Vocational Activities

	Component
Open any attachment	.74
Click any Web links	.88
Open any file via instant messenger	.78
Click a pop-up message	.63

Extraction Method: Principal Component Analysis.

For the third measure of online lifestyle, five survey items rate the computer security management measure. Respondents were asked to indicate on a 10-centimeter response line their level of agreement or disagreement with each statement. The terms *strongly agree* and *strongly disagree* anchor the response line. As discussed in the methodology section, these five items have opposite directions compared to two other online lifestyle observed variables. The structure of computer security management questionnaires indicated that higher levels of computer security management are likely to minimize computer-crime victimization. Thus, the original scale's possible aggregate range is 0 to 50, with the higher scores reflecting higher levels of computer security management.

The research hypotheses propose that the more time online users spend and the more users engage in risky behaviors in cyberspace, the greater the chance they will be victimized. Thus, each computer security management item needed to be reversely coded for fitting into the model by subtracting the values from absolute value of 10. In other words, higher values represent higher negligence of security management after the recoding process.

The psychometric properties appearing in Table 22 indicate that the recoded computer security management scale has an adequate internal consistency coefficient of .76, which is sufficient for research purposes. All five scale items (Item 1 = .42, Item 2 = .46, Item 3 = .49, and Item 4 = 68, Item 5 = .60) performed well and sufficiently met the acceptable levels of item-total correlation of .30. Thus, for research purposes, the scales had adequate item-total correlations. The mean security management score for this sample is 31.79, with a standard deviation of 11.34. The scale has a satisfactory skewness of -.52 and kurtosis of -.34. The results from skewness and kurtosis indicated that the scales have met the acceptable levels of approximate normality for SEM analysis.

Table 22

Item-Total Correlations for Cyber-security Management: Five Items

Item		Item total correlation
1.	I frequently updated my computer security software during the last 10 months.	.42
2.	I frequently changed the passwords for my e-mail accounts during the last 10 months.	.46
3	I used different passwords and user IDs for each of my Internet accounts during the last 10 months.	.49
4	I frequently checked to make sure my computer security was on before I used the Internet during the last 10 months.	.68
5.	I frequently searched for more effective computer security software during the last 10 months.	.60

Cronbach's Alpha = .76

The unidimensionality of the scales is assessed utilizing Cattell's Scree test with principal components factor analysis using a varimax rotation (see Figure 14). Table 23 presents the eigenvalues from the principal components factor analysis for each scale. The results indicated that there was one very clear factor, with an eigenvalue of

2.58, which is the most marked distinction in eigenvalues between the first and second factor. In other words, after the first factor, each of factors was not very different from the other factors that had eigenvalues below 1. An inspection of the Scree plot also shows the eigenvalues level off after the first factor. In addition, the "Component Matrix" for Factor 1 indicated all positive and relatively large values (see Table 24). This result indicated that Factor 1 was essentially the total of the responses over all five items. In other words, five items are represented as a unitary construct of computer security management.

In sum, the digital guardian scales met the basic measurement criteria for SEM. The scales had acceptable reliability, acceptable item-total correlations, acceptable skewness and kurtosis levels, and observed variables are unidimensional.

Table 23

Principal Components Analysis (Varimax Rotation) of Cyber-Security Management

Factor	Eigenvalue
1	2.58
2	.96
3	.61
4	.50
5	.35

Table 24

Component Matrix (Varimax Rotation) of Cyber-Security Management

	Component
Recoded update security	.62
Recoded change passwords	.65
Recoded change user IDs	.68
Recoded security check	.84
Recoded search effective security	.78

Extraction Method: Principal Component Analysis.

Figure 14. *Scree plot for cyber-security management items.*

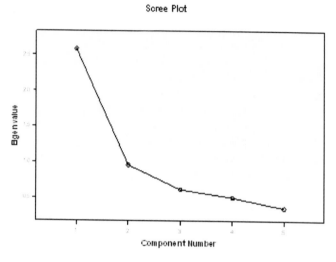

Scree Plot

CFA on Online Lifestyle

After assessment of each of the online lifestyle observed variables, CFA was reutilized to examine whether four observed online lifestyle variables show a response configuration indicative of unidimensionality. Since the factor analysis on each of online lifestyle variables had individually confirmed unidimensionality, the sum of the combination of individual item scores on each of observed variables can be analyzed via a confirmatory factor analysis (CFA). After producing four-item cumulative scales (online vocational and leisure activities, risky vocational activities, risky leisure activities, and computer security management), a confirmatory factor analysis was utilized to confirm whether the loadings of the four observed variables represent a single online lifestyle latent variable in the model. In addition, a varimax rotation was used to identify factor loadings in each variable with a single online lifestyle latent variable through an orthogonal rotation to ensure the quality of magnitude of factor loading.

Tables 25 and 26 show the online lifestyle latent structure as a set of four observed variables. The unidimensionality of the scales was confirmed by utilizing Cattell's Scree test with principal components factor analysis using varimax rotation. The results indicate that there is one very clear factor, with an eigenvalue of 1.72. After the first factors, each of factors is similar to the other factors that have eigenvalues below 1. The Scree plot also shows the eigenvalues level off after the first factor.

However, the rotated loadings in the "Component Matrix" revealed that Recoded Security Management (Value = -.42) contains relatively small loading. Communality is the sum of the squares of the factor loadings values for each variable. In addition, small communality (Value = .18) suggests that this item does not share common factors with other items. The quantity of 1- communality represents the proportion of the variable's variance attributable to the error term factor. Hence, the communality of .18 indicates that the residual error is very large. Upon further examination, correlation and covariance matrix also indicated that Recoded Security Management was not closely associated with three other online lifestyle variables (see Table 27). In sum, the low factor loading of -.42, low communality of .18, and the correlation and covariance matrix indicated that the variable is little related to other variables (see Tables 28 and 30).

Table 25
Principal Components Analysis (Varimax Rotation) of Online Lifestyle

Factor	Eigenvalue
1	1.72
2	.96
3	.74
4	.58

Figure 15. *Scree plot for online lifestyle items.*

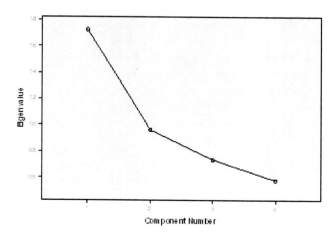

Table 26
Component Matrix (Varimax Rotation) of Online Lifestyle

	Component
OL1: Vocational & leisure activities	.78
OL2: Risky online leisure activities	.75
OL3: Risky online vocational activities	.60
OL4: Recoded security management	-.42

Table 27
Correlations between Online Lifestyle Variables

	OL1	OL2	OL3	OL4
OL1	1			
OL2	.412(**)	1		
OL3	.268(**)	.27(**)	1	
OL4	-.220(**)	-.14	-.05	1

Table 28
Communalities

	Initial	Extraction
Vocational & leisure activities	1.000	.61
Risky leisure activities	1.000	.57
Risky vocational activities	1.000	.37
Recoded security management	1.000	.18

Extraction Method: Principal Component Analysis.

After removing "Recoded Security Management," CFA based on three online lifestyle observed variables was reassessed. The reassessed online lifestyle measure appears in Tables 27 and 28, and the Catell Scree plot in Figure 16. The results indicate that excluding "Recoded Security Management" produced a clearer picture of the online lifestyle measure. An eigenvalue of 1.64 in the Scree plot validated that Factor 1 was essentially the total of the responses over all 3 items, and they are clearly represented as a single online lifestyle factor (see Tables 29 and 30). The "Component Matrix" also supported this result by indicating all positive and relatively large factor loadings (See Table 30).

Therefore, the reassessment process confirmed that the loadings of three observed variables, excluding recoded security management variable, represent online lifestyle latent variable in the model. Only three observed variables (Vocational & Leisure Activities, Risky Leisure Activities, and Risky Vocational Activities) have been taken into consideration as online lifestyle measure for SEM analysis.

Table 29
Principal Components Analysis (Varimax Rotation) of Online Lifestyle Excluding OL4

Factor	Eigenvalue
1	1.64
2	.77
3	.59

Figure 16. *Scree plot for online lifestyle items excluding OL4.*

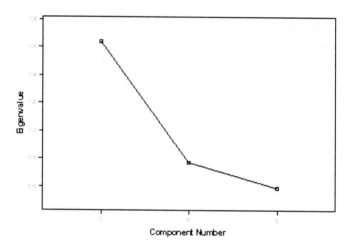

Table 30
Component Matrix (Varimax Rotation) of Online Lifestyle Excluding OL4

	Component
OL1: Vocational & leisure activities	.77
OL2: Risky online leisure activities	.80
OL3: Risky online vocational activities	.62

Extraction Method: Principal Component Analysis.

Computer-Crime Victimization

Three computer-crime victimization items have been developed for this study. Major computer crime reports tend to focus on victimization based on the private sector, and these reports clearly delineate the number of victimization occurrence, time loss, and monetary loss as major findings. Thus, the current project has adapted the construct of corporate computer-crime victimization to delineate individual-crime victimization.

Computer-crime victimization scale consists of three distinct observed variables: (a) total frequency of victimization, (b) total number of hours lost, and (c) total monetary loss. Descriptive qualities and item-total correlations of computer-crime victimization measures are shown in Tables 31 and 32. According to the findings, 59.3% of respondents out of the total population of 204 experienced at least one computer virus infection during the last 10 months (from August, 2006 to May, 2007). The average number of incidents was 3.85 based on the wide range from 0 to 250 times; 12.3% of respondents reported experiencing monetary loss on fixing computer due to computer virus infections. The average monetary loss was $17.86, and the single greatest financial loss in this survey was $700. Of those respondents that quantified the time to fix computer, 40.2% said that they spent a minimum of 1 hour fixing the computer due to virus infections, and the maximum number of hours spent fixing the computer was 100 hours during the last 10-month period.

In terms of data quality, the descriptive statistics imply conditions of severe nonnormality of data that are one of violations in SEM assumptions. Three computer-crime victimization scales contained extreme values of skewness and kurtosis, and the reliability coefficient indicated poor variability and low item scale correlations due to strong outliers (see Tables 33 and 34).

Table 31
Descriptive Qualities of Computer-Crime Victimization Measures

Name of Scale	N	M	SD	Skewness	Kurtosis
Frequency of virus infection	204	3.85	21.45	9.54	97.88
Monetary loss	204	$ 17.85	75.95	6.50	49.39
Hour loss	204	6.23 Hrs	13.69	3.89	18.33

Table 32

Item-Total Correlations for Computer-Crime Victimization

Item		Item total correlation
1.	During the last 10 months, how many times did you have computer virus infection incidents?	.28
2.	During the last 10 months, approximately how much money did you spend fixing your computer due to computer virus infections?	.24
3.	During the last 10 months, approximately how many hours were spent fixing your computer due to the virus infections?	.29

Cronbach's Alpha = .26

Kline (1998) emphasized that under conditions of severe nonnormality of data can lead to inaccuracy of model fit estimations. Even small departures from multivariate normality can produce significant differences in the chi-square test and mislead maximum likelihood estimation (MLE), which is the central method in SEM for estimating structure coefficients. Thus, utilizing transforms to normalized data are applied in order to correct nonnormally distributed data for this research.

The assessment of descriptive statistics revealed that there were strong outliers on each computer-crime victimization item. In order to adjust a highly skewed distribution to be better approximate a normal distribution, transforming from the original items, ratio level, to a Likert-scale format based on 4 possible responses (0 to 3) was applied through a recoding process by minimizing the magnitude of outliers. The research has adapted the existing scales from the 2004 Australian Computer Crime and Security Survey. Even though the survey primarily focused on private organization sectors, the adaptation of their scales should be adequate to delineate individual computer-crime victimization. In the first item, "During the last 10 months, how many times did you have computer virus infection incidents?," the original responses were coded to 0 to 3 scales (0 = 0 time, 1 = 1 – 5 times, 2 = 6 – 10 times, 3 = over 10) that are equivalent to the scales from 2004 Australian Computer Crime and Security Survey. In the second item, "During the last 10 months, approximately how much money did you spend fixing your computer due to computer virus infections?," the original responses were labeled to a scale from 0 to 3 (0 = $0, 1 = $1-50$, 2 = $51-$100, 3 = over $100). In fact, there were no specific guidelines of monetary loss in the survey, so this category of the scales was developed based on the distribution of responses from participants and the adaptation of the survey structure.

In the third item, "During the last 10 months, approximately how many hours were spent fixing your computer due to the virus infections?," the original values were transformed to a scale from 0 to 3 (0 = 0 hour, 1 = 1 -12 hours, 2 = 13 – 84 hours, 3 = over 84 hours). In the 2004 Australian Computer Crime and Security Survey (2005), the time it took to recover from the most serious incident based on day, week, and month period was estimated. The research adapted this time period by calculating 12 hours per one day for fixing computer, so scale 1, 2, and 3 respectively represent an hourly basis for days, weeks, and months.

Transforming the original values to the Likert format was necessary, because the recoding process minimized the extremely skewed distribution and high kurtosis. Hence, the adjusted items make more accurate inferences from the sample to population.

Tables 35 and 36 show new computer-crime victimization measures that reflect the Likert format. After the application of the transformation to Likert format, the values of skewness and kurtosis have significantly decreased. In addition, both Cronbach's alpha and item total correlation values have significantly improved. Even though Item 2 has a borderline of the absolute value of skewness, the shape of distribution is better approximate a normal distribution compared to previous distribution. Even though the transformation to Likert format could not achieve appropriate normal distribution, it offered the minimal acceptance of skewness and kurtosis levels for SEM analysis.

Table 33
Descriptive Qualities of Computer-Crime Victimization Measures:
Likert Format

Name of scale	N	M	SD	Skewness	Kurtosis
Frequency of virus infection	204	.65	.63	.92	1.98
Monetary loss	204	.25	.74	3	7.76
Hour loss	204	.58	.80	1.14	.27

Table 34
Item-Total Correlations for Computer-Crime Victimization: (Likert
Format)

Item		Item total correlation
1.	During the last 10 months, how many times did you have computer virus infection incidents?	.55
2.	During the last 10 months, approximately how much money did you spend fixing your computer due to computer virus infections?	.35
3.	During the last 10 months, approximately how many hours were spent fixing your computer due to the virus infections?	.53

Cronbach's Alpha = .66

As a measure of unidimensionality, the principal components factor analysis was performed via varimax rotation with a Scree test. The most evident break in the eigenvalues was between first and second factors (see Table 35). The Scree test visually inspects that the "elbow" is between the first and second factors (see Figure 17). "Component Matrix" for factor 1 also indicated that Factor 1 is essentially the total of the responses over all three items (see Table 36). Thus, the confirmatory factor analysis confirms that the computer-crime victimization measure was unidimensional.

The computer-crime victimization scales met the basic measurement criteria for SEM after the application of transformation to Likert scale. The scales have acceptable reliability (Cronbach's Alpha = .66), acceptable item-total correlations, acceptable skewness and kurtosis levels, and the observed variables are unidimensional.

Table 35
Principal Components Analysis (Varimax Rotation) of Computer-Crime Victimization

Factor	Eigenvalue
1	1.81
2	.76
3	.43

Figure 17. *Scree plot for computer-crime victimization items.*

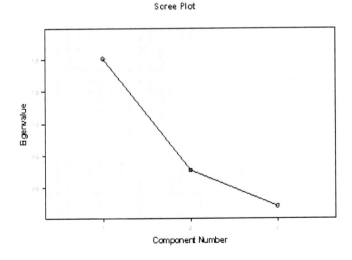

Scree Plot

Component Number

Table 36

Component Matrix (Varimax Rotation) of Computer-Crime
Victimization

	Component
CV1: Frequency of crime victimization	.84
CV2: Monetary loss	.64
CV3: Hour loss	.84

Extraction Method: Principal Component Analysis.

MEASUREMENT MODEL

As mentioned in the methodology section, the SEM analysis uses ML. ML is the most common estimation method to determine the parameters that maximize the probability of the sample data. ML generally yields estimators with good statistical properties and are statistically compatible with most modules and different types of data. In addition, ML offers quantifying unknown model properties through confidence bounds. Although the first assessment of data on computer-crime victimization items reached the abnormal levels of skewness and kurtosis for the distribution, the transformation to Likert format minimized the problem by adjusting the strong outliers to acceptable levels of skewness and kurtosis. Thus, levels of skewness and kurtosis for the distributions of digital guardian, online lifestyle, and computer-crime victimization were well below or close to respectively 3 and 10, so the research conveyed the minimum acceptable levels of skewness and kurtosis for SEM analysis.

As a next step, identification of the measurement model was assessed through computation of unique estimates for the parameters of the measurement model. There are two conditions for Confirmatory Factor Analysis (CFA) models. First, if the model is *underidentified* (there are an infinite number of possible parameter estimate values), the model would not be successfully fitted. Employing the formula presented in the method section, there were 8 observed variables, so there were $[8(8+1)]/2 = 36$ available degrees of freedom. There are 12 residual variance estimates, 1 factor covariance, 2 path coefficients, and 3 factor loadings—there are 18 parameters estimated; 36 degrees of freedom -18 estimated parameters = 18 available degrees of freedom. Thus, the model was clearly overidentified and met a satisfactory level of identification to test the proposed statistical hypotheses including a global model fit. Second, Kline (1998) asserted that each latent variable must have a scale. Since fixing one factor loading per latent variable equal to one allows fixing parameter values to know constants, the second condition is also met.

The meaning of poor fitness in model implies that factors are not sufficient to explain the items' shared variance due to poor model specification. In other words, the model cannot be valid without gaining acceptable model fitness. Nine fit indices were examined in order to determine the model fitness of the measurement model. Table 2 from Gibbs et al. (2000) indicated the fit indices, their justifications, and standards.

Five indexes of absolute fit including chi-square, adjusted chi-square, root mean square residual (RMR), root squared error of approximation (RMSEA), and global fit index (GFI) are reported (see Table 37). In addition, the Tucker-Lewis Index (TLI), the comparative fit index (CFI), the parsimonious goodness of fit (PGFI), and the Expected cross-validation (ECVI) are presented in order to measure relative fitness by comparing the specified model with the measurement model.

Three out of five measures of absolute fit (adjusted chi-square, RMSEA, and GFI) sufficiently met their standards. Since the probability value of the chi-square test was smaller than the .05 level, the test result indicates the rejection of the null hypothesis that the model fits the data. In other words, the observed covariance matrix and the measurement model covariance matrix were statistically different. However, such a rejection based on the chi-square test result was relatively less substantial compared to other descriptive fit statistics because the chi-square test is very sensitive to sample size and nonnormal distribution of the input variables (Hu & Bentler, 1999; Kline, 1998). Thus, examining other descriptive fit statistics would be of substantive interest in this project.

Even though there was no absolute RMR standard, the obtained RMR value of 1.70 appeared to be high because an RMR of 0 indicates a perfect fit. In other words, the sample variances and covariances differ from the corresponding estimated variances and covariances. The CFI and TLI, which compare the absolute fit of the specified model to the absolute fit of the measurement model, also sufficiently met the standard for appropriate model fit. Although the PGFI and ECVI do not have precise standards, the guideline of Gibbs et al. (2000) suggest that these obtained values are very close to good model fit. Kline (1998) recommended at least four descriptive fit statistics such as adjusted chi-square, GFI, TLI, and RMSEA. Despite of fact that it was very difficult to construct a model that fits well at first, the measurement model has acquired the overall good model fit. Therefore, the measurement model fits well, based on the suggested descriptive measures of fit.

The standardized and unstandardized factor loadings are shown in Figure 18. The diagram indicated that scores on the survey scales reflect two latent variables, along with the variance that is unique to each item. In order to set the scale of measurement for the latent factors and residuals, at least one of the unstandardized factor loading was fixed to a value of one. Hence, setting variances of the factors to value of one provided a scale for the factor and implicit standardized solutions. All of the regression coefficients in the model were significantly different from zero beyond the .01 level.

SEM offers researchers the ability to examine a theoretical model, along with any exogenous variables included in a model, from the standpoint of structure. The research hypotheses were constructed based on routine activities theory in order to assess computer-crime victimization and the components of the theory. SEM was used to delineate the existence of any statistical significance between the online lifestyle factor, the digital-capable guardianship factor, and levels of individual computer-crime victimization among the college student.

One of the hypotheses is that the unstandardized structural coefficient for the path from the level of digital-capable guardianship to computer-crime victimization will be statistically significant, and the standardized structural coefficient for the path will indicate a negative association. This prediction means that the lesser the number of installed computer security programs with lesser duration of having installed computer security programs, the higher the rate will be for computer-crime victimization. In other words, online users who did not install adequate computer security programs in their personal or laptop computers will experience a greater chance of being victimized. This expected finding was derived from the routine activities theoretical tenant regarding capable guardianship.

Table 37
Selected Fit Indexes for the Measurement Model

	Model Fitness	Index	Value	Standard point
1.	Absolute fit	Chi-square (χ^2)	34.47 (df = 18) P. = .011	p. > .05
2.	Absolute fit	Normal Chi-square (χ^2 / df)	1.915	< 3
3.	Absolute fit	Root mean square residual (RMR)	1.73	Close to 0
4.	Absolute fit	Root mean square error of approximation (RMSEA)	.07	< .10
5.	Absolute fit	Goodness of fit index (GFI)	.96	.90
6.	Incremental fit	Tucker-Lewis Index (TLI)	.95	Close to 1
7.	Incremental fit	Comparative fit index (CFI)	.97	Close to 1
8.	Parsimony	Parsimony goodness of fit index (PGFI)	.48	Larger value = Better fit
9.	Comparative fit	Expected cross-validation index (ECVI)	.35	Smaller value = Better fit

Figure 18. *Measurement model.*

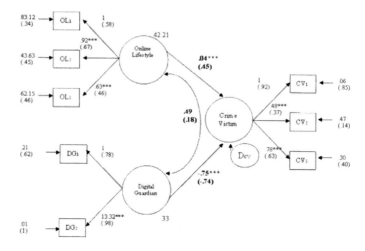

Note. The standardized coefficients, in parentheses, and unstandarized loadings above the values are shown on the paths among latent variables and observed variables. The values on the bidirectional arrow between the digital guardianship and the online lifestyle latent variable are correlations, in parentheses, and covariances above the value. Each product-moment correlation coefficient in parentheses and covariances above the values are shown left and right side on the model before each observed variable. The values near each latent variable are variances.

Standardized coefficients estimate the relative contribution of each predictor variable to each outcome variable. The results indicated that there is a significant difference between the standardized and unstandarized coefficients. This was due to the fact that variables with very different measurement scales entered into the same model results in sharp discrepancies between the standardized and unstandardized regression coefficient output.

Figure 18 indicates that the digital guardian latent variable has statistically significant unstandardized regression coefficients. The negative statistical relationship between the digital guardian and crime victimization is illustrated by the statistically significant unstandardized regression coefficient of -.75. The standardized coefficient of -.74 also reveals the digital guardian is the most substantial factor on computer-crime victimization. Among digital guardian observed variables, standardized coefficients indicate that both equipping number of computer security software and the duration of the presence of computer security software provide almost an evenly substantial impact on minimizing computer-crime victimization. These findings sufficiently support the routine activities theoretical component, capable guardianship, by emphasizing the importance of computer security that contributes to reduce computer-crime victimization.

There were three specific predictions derived from life-exposure theory based on online vocational and leisure activities, online risky activities, and the management of cyber-security that contributes to computer-crime victimization. First, the more time online users spend in cyberspace, the greater the chance they will be victimized. Second, online users who have higher risky online behaviors are more likely to be victimized. Third, online users who inadequately manage the installed computer security programs will more likely be victimized.

Based on the first prediction, the research assumed that the unstandardized structural coefficient for the path from the level of online lifestyle to computer-crime victimization will be statistically significant, and the standardized structural coefficient for the path from the level of online lifestyle to computer-crime victimization will indicate a positive effect.

The research findings indicated that the relationship between the online lifestyle factor and computer-crime victimization is strong as well. The unstandardized path coefficient of .04 revealed that a substantial, statistically significant relationship exists between the online lifestyle factor and computer-crime victimization. This finding confirms the first and second predictions. The unstandarized coefficients of online lifestyle confirmed that the online users, who spend significant time and engaged in risky online behaviors in cyberspace, are likely to be victimized. In addition, the standardized coefficient of .67 indicates that risky online leisure activities (visiting unknown websites, downloading games, music, and movies) provide the most substantial contribution to computer-crime victimization among online lifestyle category.

Unfortunately, since the computer security management variable was removed in the measurement model earlier due to the low correlation among other online lifestyle variables, the research was unable to derive the adequate findings for the third prediction. However, the findings have uncovered that online users who engage in extensive hours online and risky online behaviors are more likely to be victimized. In addition, the findings empirically support the life-exposure theoretical perspective on computer-crime victimization.

The researcher also hypothesized that there will be an interaction effect among two factors, digital-capable guardianship and online lifestyle, and this effect will directly contribute to the level of computer-crime victimization. Surprisingly, the results indicated that there was little correlation among two latent variables. Although the covariance between digital guardian and online lifestyle indicator suggested positive covariance, the result was insignificant ($p = .056$). In other words, the research uncovered that there was no interaction effect between personal online lifestyle and equipping computer security features on personal desktop or laptop computers.

In sum, the research provide empirical supports on the components of routine activities theory, which delineate the existence of statistical significance among the online lifestyle factor, the digital-capable guardianship factor, and the levels of individual crime victimization based on the college student sample. More precisely, computer-crime victims are more susceptible to personal computer victimization compared to other online users who have fully installed computer security programs, or who use the Internet less and who avoid risky online behaviors.

STRUCTURAL MODEL

Table 38 shows the fit of the structural model using the same nine descriptive fit indexes for previously testing the fit of the measurement model. Similar to the measurement model, the probability value of the chi-square test (p. = .005) was less than the .05 level. The test result indicated the rejection of the null hypothesis that the model fits the data. As stated in the measurement model, such a rejection based on the chi-square test result appeared to be due to sample size. Thus, examining other descriptive fit statistics would be of substantive interest in this research.

Similar to the measurement model, three measures of absolute fit (adjusted chi-square, RMSEA, and GFI) met or exceeded their standards. The obtained RMR value of 3.03 was higher than measurement model that indicated the structural model did not offer a perfect fit. The CFI and TLI values were similar to the measurement model, which sufficiently met the standard for appropriate model fit. The PGFI and ECVI values were also similar to the measurement model that suggested an adequate fit for the model. Although the structural model was unable to convey an adequate fit for model compared to the measurement model, the model had acquired the overall good model fit for the purposes of the research.

Figure 19. *Structural model.*

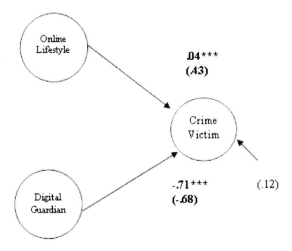

Table 38
Selected Fit Indexes for the Measurement Model

	Model Fitness	Index	Value	Standard Point
1.	Absolute fit	Chi-square (χ^2)	38.392 (df = 19) P. = .005	p. > .05
2.	Absolute fit	Normal Chi-square (χ^2 / df)	2.02	< 3
3.	Absolute fit	Root mean square residual (RMR)	3.03	Close to 0
4.	Absolute fit	Root mean square error of approximation (RMSEA)	.07	< .10
5.	Absolute fit	Goodness of fit index (GFI)	.96	.90
6.	Incremental fit	Tucker-Lewis Index (TLI)	.94	Close to 1
7.	Incremental fit	Comparative fit index (CFI)	.96	Close to 1
8.	Parsimony	Parsimony goodness of fit index (PGFI)	.50	Larger value = Better fit
9.	Comparative fit	Expected cross-validation index (ECVI)	.36	Smaller value = Better fit

The structural model delineates potential causes of computer-crime victimization by empirically supporting the adopted tenets of Cohen and Felson's routine activities theory and Hindelang, Gottfredson, and Garofalo's life-exposure theory. Specific predictions, which the level of digital guardianship and the level of online lifestyle have significant influences on computer-crime victimization, were supported in this sample using these measures.

The unstandardized structural coefficient for the path from the level of digital-capable guardian to computer-crime victimization (-.71) is statistically significant at the .001 level, and the standardized structural coefficient for the path indicates a negative association. This result means that the lesser the number of installed computer security programs with the lesser duration, the higher the rate will be for computer-crime victimization. In other words, online users who do not install computer security programs in their personal or laptop computers will experience a greater chance of being victimized. This finding provides support for the routine activities theoretical tenant regarding capable guardianship.

The unstandardized structural coefficient for the path from the level of online lifestyle to computer-crime victimization (.04) was also statistically significant at the .001 level, and the direction of the standardized structural coefficient indicated a positive effect. The findings uncovered that online users, who engage in using extensive hours online, and who have risky online behaviors were more likely to be victimized. Similar to the measurement model, the findings provided empirical supports for Hindelang, Gottfredson, and Garofalo's life-exposure theory.

RELATIONSHIP BETWEEN DEMOGRAPHIC VARIABLES AND RISK FACTORS OF COMPUTER CRIME VICTIMIZATION

In criminology literature, it is commonly acknowledged that demographic factors such as age and gender are associated with general crime victimization in physical worlds (Cohen et al., 1981; Gottfredson, 1984, 1986; Laub, 1990). However, the relationship between social context variables and factors associated with individual computer crime victimization has not precisely revealed.

One of main interests in this research was to examine how demographics variables interact with factors of computer crime victimization. The assessment of social context factors in cyber spatial structures is crucial because the research assumes that social environments also constantly interact with the traits of online spatiality.

Demographic Variables vs. Fear of Cybercrime

The respondents were asked to identify the most fearful cybercrime in the survey (See Appendix B). Six different categories of cybercrime were offered as well as an "Other" category. While 1% of respondents reported cyber-harassment as the least fearful crime, over 60% of the survey participants chose identify theft as the most fearful cyber-crime. As expected, hacking was also fairly high on the list of cybercrime categories with 28%. Interestingly, only 2.5% reported Internet fraud and 3.4% reported online stalking as the most fearful crimes within the category (see Table 39).

In the physical world, the assessment of demographic variables revealed that gender, age, and race variables play a substantial role in determining the level of fear. This research applied various statistical methods to estimate causal relationship between three demographic variables and fear of cybercrime; however, the research findings indicated that gender was found only to be a significant predictor on fear of cybercrime.

Table 39
Fear of Cybercrime

Cybercrime categories	Frequency (f)	Percentage (%)
Internet fraud	5	2.5
Identity theft	130	63.7
Hacking	57	27.9
Online stalking	7	3.4
Cyber-harassment	2	1.0
Other	3	1.5
Total (N)	204	100.0

Figure 20. *Fear of cybercrime bar chart*

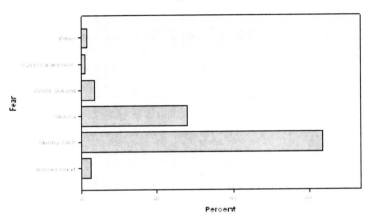

The chi-square test is a method to determine if two variables are independent of one another in nominal bivariate analyses. Since two variables, gender and the cybercrime categories, are nominal levels, the chi-square test was used to determine whether gender difference is statistically significant in identifying the most fearful cyber-crime among the six different crime categories.

In terms of percent within gender, females have a greater fear of identity theft (66.1%) and online stalking (6.3%), compared to 61% and 0% of males, respectively (see Table 40). While 33% of males had identified hacking, 24% of female respondents indicated it as the most fearful crime (see Table 41). The results of the Chi-square test verified the significant relationship between gender and identified the most fearful cybercrime from online users' perspectives (p. < .05). Since the chi-square test suggest a statistical significant relationship between two variables, applying Cramer's V was necessary to determine the magnitude of nominal association. Cramer's V is a chi-square based on measure of association for tables larger than 2 X 2 (Bachman & Paternoster, 2004). In the findings, the magnitude of the Cramer's V of .242 indicated that about 24.2% of the variation in identifying the most fearful cybercrime is accounted for by gender difference (see Table 42).

In sum, research findings suggest that identity theft was ranked as the most fearful cybercrime category and gender difference only differentially contributes to perceived risk of cybercrime among other demographic variables.

Table 40
Fear * Gender Crosstabulation

			Gender	
			Male	Female
Fear	Internet fraud	Count	4	1
		Expected Count	2.3	2.7
		% within Gender	4.3%	.9%
	Identity theft	Count	56	74
		Expected Count	58.6	71.4
		% within Gender	60.9%	66.1%
	Hacking	Count	30	27
		Expected Count	25.7	31.3
		% within Gender	32.6%	24.1%
	Online stalking	Count	0	7
		Expected Count	3.2	3.8
		% within Gender	.0%	6.3%
	Cyber-harassment	Count	0	2
		Expected Count	.9	1.1
		% within Gender	.0%	1.8%
	Other	Count	2	1
		Expected Count	1.4	1.6
		% within Gender	2.2%	.9%
Total		Count	92	112
		Expected Count	92.0	112.0
		% within Gender	100.0%	100.0%

Table 41
Chi-Square Tests

	Value	Df	Asymp. sig. (2-sided)
Pearson chi-square	11.937(a)	5	.036
Likelihood ratio	15.438	5	.009
N of valid cases	204		

a 8 cells (66.7%) have expected count less than 5. The minimum expected count is .90.

Table 42
Symmetric Measures

		Value	Approx. sig.
Nominal by nominal	Cramer's V	.242	.036
N of valid cases		204	

a Not assuming the null hypothesis.
b Using the asymptotic standard error assuming the null hypothesis.

Demographic Variables vs. Main Factors in Computer Crime Victimization

This section presents how demographic variables (race, age, and gender) relate to main factors in computer crime victimization (capable guardianship, online lifestyle, and computer crime victimization), which are the major constructs in this research. In order to delineate significant relationships between demographic variables and the suggested main factors, different statistical analyses were applied by taking into consideration the scales of the variables.

First, the research examined the statistical relationship between race and observed variables based on the suggested three factors. Anderson (1972) asserts that advantage of utilizing Fisher's LSD (Least Significant Difference) is that "it can be easily applied to any fixed effects linear model, be it analysis of variance, regression, or analysis of covariance" (p. 30). Prior to utilizing LSD test, one-way ANOVA (analysis of variance) was used to test for determining the population means based on race are not equal as a first step. It was hypothesized that there is variability in the population based on race, which contributes to the level of digital guardianship, online lifestyle, and computer crime victimization. The F statistic offers the researcher an estimate the existence of group variability among the observed variables. If the F-test rejects the null hypothesis of equal means, then Fisher's LSD (Least Significant Difference) can be used to compare group means.

Table 43
Descriptives: Race vs. Computer Crime Victimization

		N	Mean	SD	Std. error
Frequency	African American	15	.73	.46	.12
	Asian	4	.50	.58	.29
	Caucasian	172	.65	.65	.05
	Hispanic	4	.75	.50	.25
	Other	9	.44	.73	.24
	Total	204	.65	.63	.04
Monetary loss	African American	15	.20	.78	.20
	Asian	4	1.50	1.73	.87
	Caucasian	172	.22	.68	.05
	Hispanic	4	.00	.00	.00
	Other	9	.33	1.00	.33
	Total	204	.25	.74	.05
Hour loss	African American	15	.73	.88	.23
	Asian	4	.75	.96	.48
	Caucasian	172	.52	.71	.05
	Hispanic	4	.25	.50	.25
	Other	9	.22	.44	.15
	Total	204	.53	.71	.05

The results from the F statistic indicate that there were no significant differences in observed variables based on capable guardianship and online lifestyle among the groups. However, an ANOVA analysis showed that race has a significant difference in monetary loss category, which is one of three computer crime victimization observed variables at the .05 level (see Table 44). The results at the .05 significance level using Fisher's LSD test suggested that Asian students tend to experience higher monetary loss compared to other racial groups (see Table 45). The results can also be visually seen in Figure 21.

Table 44
ANOVA

		Sum of squares	Df	Mean square	F	Sig.
Frequency of crime victimizati on	Between groups	.613	4	.153	.38 1	.82 2
	Within groups	79.975	199	.402		
	Total	80.588	203			
Monetary loss	Between Groups	6.740	4	1.685	3.1 94	.01 4*
	Within groups	105.005	199	.528		
	Total	111.745	203			
Hour loss	Between groups	1.982	4	.495	.97 7	.42 1
	Within groups	100.896	199	.507		
	Total	102.877	203			

*Significance at a .05 level

Table 45
Multiple Comparisons: LSD

Dependent variable	(I) Race	(J) Race	Mean difference (I-J)	Std. Error	Sig.
Monetary loss	Asian	African American	1.30000(*)	.40877	.002
		Caucasian	1.27907(*)	.36740	.001
		Hispanic	1.50000(*)	.51364	.004
		Other	1.16667(*)	.43651	.008

* The mean difference is significant at the .05 level.

Figure 21. *Race vs. monetary loss*

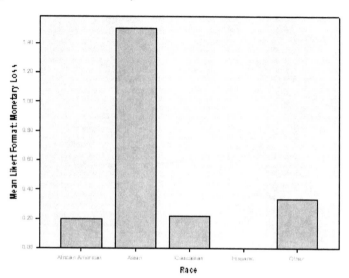

Fisher's LSD method, which was based on the previous rejection of the null hypothesis with F test, indicated that racial difference significantly contributes to the level of monetary loss.

.Second, the research also examined the statistical association between age difference and observed variables based on the suggested three factors. In order to examine whether age has a substantial impact on the level of individual online lifestyle, capable guardianship, and crime victimization, Ordinary Least Squares (OLS) regression analysis was applied. Since SEM assumptions were previously checked, the research naturally assumed that the regression assumptions were not being violated. Three specific hypotheses were tested in order to measure how age difference has substantial influences on the level of digital capable guardianship, individual online lifestyle, and computer crime victimization.

In the first hypothesis, the unstandarized coefficients of -.044 and -.470 indicated that age has negative, substantial impacts on the level of digital capable guardianship (p. <.05). This result suggests that individuals with older age are less likely to equip the number of computer security software with less duration (See Table 46). However, based on the R-Square, only 3% of the variation in the dependent variable can be explained by age difference (see Table 46). There is a weak, negative significant relationship between age and the level of digital capable guardianship. In other words, as age increases, the level of capable guardianship decreases, but the magnitude of this association is weak.

In the second hypothesis, online lifestyle was assessed by taking account into age difference via OLS analysis. Among four observed variables including computer security management observed variable, which was excluded in SEM assessment, the results found that age difference significantly contributes to two observed online lifestyle variables; the level of online vocational and leisure activities and risky vocational activities (p. <.05). The unstandardized coefficients of -.926 and -.505 indicate that age has a negative influence on individual vocational and leisure activities and risky vocational activities (see Table 47). R-square of .072 and .022 indicate that there are weak magnitude of associations between age and two online lifestyle observed variables (See Table 47).

Table 46
Age vs. Digital Capable Guardianship

Age (IV)	Number of security	Duration of having security
Intercept	3.510	31.881
B	-.044	-.470
p.	.000*	.021*
R square	.026	.026

*Significance at a .05 level

Table 47
Age vs. Online Lifestyle

Age (IV)	Vocational & leisure activities	Risky vocational activities
Intercept	53.012	23.523
B	-.926	-.505
p.	.000*	.032*
R square	.072	.022

*Significance at a .05 level

Hence, older online users were less likely to spend extensive time for vocational and leisure activities, and they were also less likely to engage in risky vocational activities. However, the magnitude of association was fairly weak.

In the third hypothesis, age difference significantly contributes to the level of monetary loss for fixing the computer due to computer virus infections (see Table 48). The unstandardized coefficient of .039 indicates that online users with older age are likely to spend more money to fix their computer due to the virus infections compared to younger online users (p. < .05). The R-square of .019 suggests that approximately 98% of the variation in dependent variable cannot be explained by age difference. In other words, age difference has a significant impact on the monetary loss, but the magnitude of association is very weak.

Table 48
Age vs. Computer Crime Victimization

Age (IV)	Monetary loss
Intercept	-.557
B	.039
p.	.046*
R square	.019

*Significance at a .05 level

Third, the research inspected the statistical relationship between gender and observed variables based on the suggested three factors. The *t* test was utilized to determine if there was a statistical difference between the means of male and female groups in this study. The results from the independent samples t-test indicate that gender difference contributes to the level of risky leisure activities, risky vocational activities, and security management. Since the significance of the F test (Sig. >.05) in the online activities complies the variances for male and female groups are equal, examining the "Equal Variances are assumed" row should be used to interpret the significance of the t-value (see Table 49).

Table 49
Independent Samples t-Test

		F	Sig.	t	Df	Sig. (2-tailed)	Mean Diff.
						Levene's Test	
Risky leisure activities	Equal variances assumed	3.762	.054	4.05	202	.000*	4.91
	Equal variances not assumed			3.99	177.80	.000	4.91
Risky vocational activities	Equal variances assumed	1.259	.263	-2.50	202	.013*	-3.09
	Equal variances not assumed			-2.53	200.19	.012	-3.09
Recoded security management	Equal variances assumed	.236	.672	-2.822	202	.005*	-4.43
	Equal variances not assumed			-2.849	199.88	.005	-4.43

Significance at a .05 level

In risky leisure activities, the *t* value of 4.05 and the Sig. (2-tailed) column in the p-value (*p* = .000) is less than .05 suggest that the average risky leisure activities score of male (*M* = 18.72, *SD* = 9.41) is significantly different from that of female (*M* = 13.81, *SD* = 7.89). In other words, males are more likely to engage in online risky leisure activities such as visiting unknown Web sites, downloading free games, free music, and free movies than females.

On the other hand, the *t* value of -2.5 and the Sig. (2-tailed) column in the p-value (*p* = .013) is less than .05 suggest that the average risky vocational activities score of male (*M* = 11.51, *SD* = 8.26) is significantly less that of female (*M* = 14.60, *SD* = 9.17). This finding suggests that compared to males, females tend to open any attachment in the e-mail, click on any web-links in the e-mails, open any file though the instant messenger, and click on a pop-up message that interested them.

As discussed in the methods section, security management items was reversely coded for gaining the same directions with other online lifestyle variables. Thus, higher values represent higher negligence of security management. In recoded security management, the results indicate that there is a statistically significant difference in the level of security management between males and females, t (202) = -2.82, p = .005. That is, the average recoded security management score of males (M = 29.36, SD = 10.56) is significantly less than that of females (M = 33.79, SD = 11.61) (see Table 50). In other words, males are more likely to update computer security, change the passwords for e-mail account, search for more effective computer security software, check the operation of computer security online, and use different passwords and user IDs for their Internet accounts than females.

Table 50
Group Statistics

	Gender	N	Mean	SD	Std. Error Mean
Risky leisure activities	Male	92	18.72	9.41	.98
	Female	112	13.81	7.89	.75
Risky vocational activities	Male	92	11.51	8.28	.86
	Female	112	24.60	9.17	.97
Recoded security management	Male	92	29.36	10.56	1.10
	Female	112	33.79	11.61	1.10

CHAPTER 5

Managing Computer Crime and Future Research

Cohen and Felson's (1979) routine activities theory and Hindelang, Gottfredson and Garofalo's (1978) lifestyle-exposure theory have been widely applied to explain various types of criminal victimization, and various studies have provided empirical support. The purpose of this study was to empirically estimate patterns of computer-crime victimization by applying routine activities theory. The main concepts from life-exposure theory, lifestyle variables, and one of the three major tenets from routine activities theory, "capable guardianship" were theoretically identified as two distinctive factors that play a major role against computer-crime victimization. This study conveys three specific significant contributions to the empirical literature in criminology. First, this study attempts to empirically test individual computer-crime victimization via a theoretical approach using routine activities theory. Second, utilizing structural SEM facilitates the assessment of the new theoretical model by conveying an overall picture of the relationship among the causal factors (the level of individual's computer-oriented lifestyle and the level of presence ofinstalled computer security in a computer) in the proposed model. Finally, research empirically assessed statistical relationships between demographic variables and the causal factors of computer crime. This chapter presents the findings, the key implications of these findings, the limitations of this study, and some suggestions for future studies.

In this project, the conceptual model derived from Cohen and Felson's (1979) routine activities theory and Hindelang et al.'s (1978) lifestyle-exposure theory was empirically assessed via routine activities theory's major concept, the target-hardening strategy, which is represented as digital-capable guardianship and lifestyle-exposure theory's core concept, vocational and leisure activities, which is suggested as online lifestyle. The findings here offer further empirical support for the model derived from two theories. Before discussing the overall findings, the measurement of the variables needs to be considered.

In testing the theory, the operationalization of digital-capable guardianship, online lifestyle, and computer-crime victimization was taken as a first step. SEM normally requires three observed variables of each latent variable for an optimal analysis. In this study, digital-capable guardianship has two independent scales, and online lifestyle has three independent scales that serve as their observed variables. The three observed variables that measure computer-crime victimization are constructed. It is acknowledged that having two independent scales for digital guardian latent variable does not convey optimal analysis, so it is necessary to develop multiple measures of the construct on digital guardianship for future refining of the research.

In the case of digital-capable guardianship, the measures have acceptable levels of reliability and indicators suggest they are adequate measures of the concept of digital-capable guardianship. Cronbach's alpha, item-total correlation, and the Scree test assess the reliability and unidimensional properties of the index. Although the number of computer security measure is in the undesirable range of Cronbach's alpha, the items-total correlations are respectable. The research also examined the duration of having security as a second observed variable. The results found that the scale has an adequate internal consistency coefficient and item-total correlations. The measures of capable digital guardianship were assessed for unidimensionality via confirmatory factor analysis (CFA). The Scree tests for the number of computer security scale and the duration of having security scale indicate that they are unidimensional measures. The capable digital guardianship measure's Scree test reutilizing CFA also indicates two observed variables are constructed as a unidimensional trait.

However, significant changes were made to existing measures in online lifestyle and computer-crime victimization. In the case of online lifestyle, three significant changes were made based on the assessment of reliability and validity. First, one out of nine survey items was excluded from the model in the category of online vocational and leisure activities because the item did not share much variance with other items. Second, one out of nine survey items was removed from the model based on the category of online risky activities due to a low item total correlation. In addition, the assessment of reliability test and factor analysis identified that there were two distinctive subcategories within the category, so the first subcategory of online risky activities was individually assessed with one set of four items as "online risky leisure activities," and the second subcategory was also separately assessed with one set of four items as "online risky vocational activities." Thus, after the assessment, the model included two observed variables (online risky leisure activities and online risky vocational activities) rather than having one observed variable as "online risky activities." Third, even though five survey items based on the computer security management scale provided adequate reliability, item-total correlations, acceptable skewness and kurtosis levels, and unidimensional construct, CFA revealed that the computer security management variable is little related to other online lifestyle variables, so the security management scale was excluded in order to obtain an adequate measurement model. Therefore, three observed variables (vocational and leisure activities, risky leisure activities, and risky vocational activities) were taken into consideration as the online lifestyle measure for SEM analysis. Since the findings revealed that the computer security management variable was not a part of the online lifestyle factor, the research acknowledged that considering the computer security management variable as a separate independent variable might be necessary in order to resolve this issue for future research.

In this study, three measures of computer-crime victimization were used to measure the validity of the construct: (a) total frequency of victimization, (b) total number of hours lost, and (c) total monetary loss. However, in the case of computer-crime victimization, one significant change was made based on findings from the descriptive statistics, which imply conditions of severe nonnormality of data. In order to adjust a highly skewed distribution to be close to a normal distribution, transforming from the original ratio level items to a Likert-scale format was applied through a recoding process to minimize the magnitude of outliers for each of the observed variables.

After making the adjustments described above, a number of statistical tests were performed to reassess the reliability and validity of these measures. In the case of both online lifestyle and computer-crime victimization, support was found for both reliability and validity.

In the online lifestyle measure, the vocational and leisure activities scale, risky online vocational activities scale, and risky online leisure activities scale had acceptable reliability, acceptable item item-total correlations, and they were unidimensional measures, as well. In addition, CFA reconfirmed that these observed variables are a unitary construct.

In the computer-crime victimization measure, after the application of the transformation to Likert format, the values of skewness and kurtosis significantly decreased. In addition, the significant improvements on Cronbach's alpha and item total correlation values that offer adequate acceptance for SEM analysis were found. The principal components factor analysis via varimax rotation with a Scree test also indicated that each of scales is constructed with a single underlying dimension for computer-crime victimization.

This study assessed a new theoretical model that is theoretically derived from Hindelang et al.'s (1978) lifestyle-exposure theory and Cohen and Felson's (1979) routine activities theory. The central conceptual model is that digital-capable guardianship and online lifestyle directly influence computer-crime victimization. Comparisons of structural coefficients and measures of fit indicated that the central measurement model of this study is superior over the structural model.

In general, the findings of this study provide empirical support for major theoretical elements in two traditional victimization theories, which entail empirical prediction. From routine activities theory, the researcher hypothesized the degree of installed major computer security software differentiates the rate of computer-crime victimization. The findings provided support for this proposition by indicating the higher the number of installed computer security programs with the higher duration, the lesser the rate of computer crime that will occur. From lifestyle-exposure theory, the researcher posited three specific propositions. First, the more time online users spend in cyberspace, the greater the chance they will be victimized. Second, online users who have higher risky online behaviors are more likely to be victimized. Third, online users who inadequately manage the installed computer security programs will more likely be victimized. Even though the findings offer empirical supports for the first and second propositions, the researcher was unable to make any statistical conclusion on the third proposition because the computer security management variable was removed from the model due to its low correlation with other online lifestyle variables, which would distort the statistical findings.

The study also assessed the relationship between demographic variables and computer crime victimization factors. Descriptive statistics suggested that identity theft was identified as the most fearful cybercrime category and gender was only a significant variable to determine the perceived risk of cybercrime among demographic variables. In addition, ANOVA and Fisher's LSD (Least Significant Difference) test confirmed that racial difference has a substantial impact on monetary loss in computer crime victimization. Results from OLS (Ordinary Least Squares) regression suggested that age difference has a significant influence on the level of digital capable guardianship and online lifestyle. Furthermore, the Independent samples t-test indicated that gender difference substantially contributes to the degree of engagement of risky leisure activities and risky vocational activities in cyberspace, and the level of computer security management.

In sum, the findings from this study provide an overall picture of the relationship among computer security, online lifestyle, and individual computer-crime victimization. This study adds to the growing body of computer-crime research by using SEM. In addition, this study also makes a significant contribution because it empirically tests individual computer-crime victimization by constructing innovative measurement and structural models. Most other studies on computer-crime victimization are limited because they tend to focus on private business sectors, not the individual level, and tend to provide descriptive statistical results, which are unable to convey a causal relationship between main causal factors and computer-crime victimization. Even though this study still needs to develop more precise measurements to delineate true computer-crime victimization patterns, the measurement model would facilitate other researchers exploring this potential area of criminology research by establishing an initial empirical foundation. The next section addresses the implications of these findings and offers ideas for future research.

POLICY IMPLICATIONS

Criminological theory and criminal justice policy have an indispensable relationship. According to Surtherland (1947), criminology is the body of knowledge that regards crime as a social phenomenon. It includes the process of making laws, breaking laws, and enforcing law. The criminal justice policy and practices are strongly related to this process, especially the process of making law and enforcing law. In fact, the direction of criminological theory guides empirical research, and if the research supports the theory based on empirical validity, the theory often turns into criminal justice policy.

The findings from this empirical study suggest that college students who overlook their computer oriented lifestyle in cyberspace or who neglect the presence of computer security software in their computer are likely to be victimized. The results revealed differential lifestyle patterns directly link with the occurrence of criminal victimization in cyberspace. In addition, this research supports the conclusion that the presence of computer security is the most crucial component to protect the computer systems from computer criminals. MaQuade (2006) stated that "routine activities theory has important implications for understanding crimes committed with or prevented with computers, other IT devices, or information systems" (p. 147). In other words, computer-crime victimization can be significantly minimized through abiding by adequate online lifestyle and equipping computer security technology. This section presents the importance of establishing the computer crime prevention program, which is mainly derived from the suggested research findings.

The findings suggest that establishing prosocial views of promoting adequate online lifestyle and utilizing efficient computer security will contribute to the reduction in computer-crime victimization. Even though self-directed decisions by computer users for acquiring adequate online lifestyle and installed computer security on their computers have become increasingly important, contemporary criminal justice crime prevention programs tend to neglect the importance of these issues. In addition, while the number of computer users is increasing every day, structured computer-crime prevention programs are not fully available to online users. Computer-crime prevention programs, however, can be logically categorized as school-based crime prevention programs. In fact, some colleges and universities currently offer introductory and specialized courses in computer crime and information security issues (McQuade, 2006). The primary goal of the computer-crime prevention program is to minimize potential computer-crime victimization based on educational setting. The school should be the setting for initial exposure and training in this program because many school crime prevention programs already offer specific guidelines that establish responsibilities for students in the classroom and community at large. Gottfredson et al. (1993) asserted that "interventions to establish norms and expectations for behavior" are some of the most effective strategies in the school crime prevention program (p. 145). This statement matches the general strategy and goals of the computer-crime prevention program. Numerous studies suggest that social context factors have a significant influence on crime victimization. In other words, when we educate students with an adequately structured computer-crime prevention program, the beneficial outcomes should be expected by establishing individuals' appropriate online lifestyle and building their own protections on the usage of computer.

Duke (1989) emphasized that a school environment that promotes shared values and expectation can positively influence behaviors. Changes in the school and classroom environment can clarify behavioral norms through school and discipline management intervention (Gottfredson et al., 2004). These existing effective school programs establish norms and adjust expectations for illegal or delinquent behaviors. In terms of computer-crime prevention application, the combination of computer security awareness programs and school campaigns against computer crime would facilitate changing individual online lifestyle via the social environment at school if the program is adequately constructed and implemented. McQuade (2006) asserts that a major opportunity to minimize computer crime through enhanced information security is via "public awareness, formal education, and professional training" (p. 487). The program should not only address specific methods such as general knowledge on information security and valuable tips to avoid crime victimization to help prevent computer crime, but also it should emphasize law and regulations relating to cybercrime to facilitate the acquisition of solid ethical standards for students.

The computer-crime prevention program must offer students efficient practices for safeguarding information, including the use of strong passwords and effective password management, frequent updating of antimalware definitions; installation and use of a software or hardware firewalls; regularly downloading security and other patches for operating systems and applications; installation and frequent use of antispyware and antiadware applications; backing up data systematically and in different ways; using antikeylogger, encryption, and digital signature technology. (McQuade, 2006, p. 453)

In addition, the program must employ adequate online lifestyles by alerting the individual to online risk-taking behaviors that allow students to transform the constructed general online practices into their personal lifestyles. Furthermore, the program should emphasize law and regulations on computer crime with the goal of reinforcing ethical norms and expectations for computer users' behaviors.

As the computer technology evolves every day, the level of complexities related to computer crime and information security management challenges (McQuade, 2006). There are only a few empirical studies available regarding the issue of computer crime. Thus, it is essential to develop and research computer crime related topics in order to manage future computer crime. As noted in the literature review, motivated offenders and suitable targets frequently collide in cyberspace. This happens because target suitability in cyberspace is a fully given situation due to the fact that personal information on the computer naturally carries valuable information into cyberspace that constantly attracts computer criminals. In addition, as technology advances and computer criminals become more sophisticated, law enforcement is likely to find prevention from computer crimes to be difficult. Fortunately, informal social control agents are slowly recognizing the seriousness of computer crime even if they are not actively operative in our cyber society. Thus, implementation of computer-crime prevention programs should become a part of building strong informal social control agents to strengthen existing effective guardianship through an effective education method.

It is also important to recognize that effective computer-crime prevention cannot be accomplished solely through the proposed program. A formal system of capable guardianship is also necessary to protect computer users from computer crime. Australian law enforcement strategy on computer crime emphasized issues such as "training and education; development and retention; and information and intelligence exchange" (Etter, 2001, p. 9). Carter and Katz (1997) point out that "decision makers in business, government, and law enforcement must develop policies, methods, and regulations to detect incursions, investigate and prosecute the perpetrators, and prevent future crimes" (p. 12). Fortunately, government has a fundamental interest and role in preventing computer crime by collectively working with both private and nonprofit sectors, and international agencies.

As a macro approach, changing social perceptions toward computer abusers is also essential. The media generally do not provide detailed coverage of computer crime and often eulogize hackers' activities. The New York Times reported that "bright youngsters who breach computer security should receive commendation, not condemnation" (Pfuhl, 1987, p. 121). Because there is little stigma attached to their activities, hackers rarely think of themselves as real criminals, even though they may be prosecuted and convicted of committing computer crimes.

Therefore, it is necessary to change both the social environment and individual environment for those who are in a position to engage in these activities in order to manage future computer crime. This goal can be accomplished through the implementation of an effective computer-crime prevention programs by informing effective cyber security, encouraging safe online lifestyles, increasing the level of formal and informal guardianship, and eliminating favorable or ambiguous perceptions about computer criminals. In the next section, the limitations and directions for future research based on this research will be discussed.

LIMITATIONS AND DIRECTIONS FOR FUTURE RESEARCH

This study has a number of obvious limitations that should be considered for future research. The current research included another set of research questionnaires, which consists of individual online lifestyle measures focused on the usage of public computers, such as those in the university computer labs or in cyber-cafés. The structure of the research questionnaires focused solely on personal computer or laptop ownership and usage. It is important to recognize the difference between personally-owned computer usage and public computer usage in this research. Since this research solely focused on computer-crime victimization based on online users who own their computer, and experience computer-crime victimization in their own computer, the analysis of computer-crime victimization based on public computer usage was excluded.

As a first limitation, it is difficult to delineate individual computer-crime victimization based on public computer use because multiple users normally share the same computers and are less likely to recognize their victimization. Thus, it is crucial that future research should include another set of questionnaires that are focused solely on public computer usage in order to differentiate the victimization levels on those computers. In addition, the assessment of the potential difference in online behaviors between people who use public computers versus their own computers would produce a broader and more detailed picture of individual computer-crime victimization in future research.

As stated in the sampling section, generalizability is a significant concern in this research because the student sample population is derived from only one state university in Pennsylvania. Even though the results from this study may represent the university student population, such results should not be extended as representative for the entire Pennsylvania state university population, or the university population in the United States. Such a generalization would be a reverse ecological fallacy, indicating a biased sampling. Thus, in future studies a researcher would need to identify and sample various universities. Each university should be surveyed regarding the potential correlations between online lifestyles, capable digital guardianship, and the overall level of computer-crime victimization among the university population in the United States.

In addition, the potential universities for future research should be selected by taking into consideration the level of computer technical support and the size of the student populations. Therefore, future research needs to include diverse sites that are carefully examined to ensure that the geographic locations and characteristics of the student population represent the entire university population in the United States.

An additional limitation in this study is that it is impossible to have a completely precise measure of computer security. As stated in summary in this chapter, it is fully acknowledged that having two independent scales for digital guardian latent variable does not convey an optimal analysis. Development regarding multiple measures of the construct on digital guardianship in future research is essential to convey more precise details on computer security. It is also important to acknowledge that there might be some error associated with the measurement of digital guardianship. This is due to the fact that most participants might not remember how long such computer security products had been loaded on their computers. In future studies, the researcher must be aware of this issue, and prior to the general survey administration, identifying specific dates of individual computer security installations from participants' computer systems would be crucial in order to enhance the quality of computer security measurement.

The research also concerned content validity regarding computer security. It is possible that the participants in the study might not fully understand each of the computer security definitions or precise functions of the computer security software. This lack of understanding could lead to underreporting or over-reporting. Thus, this lack of understanding would affect the content validity of the study. However, steps have been taken here to increase the precision of measurement regarding these components by providing the participants with the presurvey guideline, but even that precaution is not infallible. In future studies as well, even if the participants are given a presurvey guideline such as the one used in this study, those participants may not fully understand each of the computer security definitions or precise functions of the computer security software.

Unfortunately, the research was unable to convey any conclusion or causal relationship between the computer security management variable and computer-crime victimization because the computer security management variable was removed from the model due to its low correlation with other online lifestyle variables. Interestingly, the correlations between computer security management variable and other online lifestyle suggested that online users, who vigorously engage in online activities, tend to manage their computer security. However, this negative relationship, which is the opposite of what is stated in the research hypothesis, was very weak. The computer crime related literature asserts that this component is important to determine the computer-crime victimization. The findings from this research suggest that the future research should consider the computer security management variable as a separate independent variable. In order to delineate the potential relationship between computer security management and computer crime victimization, adding diverse computer security management scales such as measures of the usage of antikeylogger and encryption technology would be essential. Thus, it is necessary to develop more refined survey instruments to estimate this component.

In sum, researchers in future studies need to develop more precise scales to measure computer security and online users' behaviors for delineating a true crime victimization model. Thus, future research must remain cognizant of this fact and apply the same, if not more, protection to ensure this aspect of content validity.

FUTURE DIRECTIONS ON COMPUTER CRIME PREVENTION PROGRAM

Prevention is the preferred strategy for dealing with crime, but there are few cyber-crime prevention programs in existence. Few existing cyber-crime prevention programs have been empirically evaluated. The policy implication section briefly introduced a computer-crime prevention program, which was mainly derived from routine activities theory.

In order to construct an effective computer crime prevention program, it is imperative to reflect on other theoretical perspectives that would convey positive effects on deterring potential computer crime. Recent criminological literature links illegal computer crime activities to social learning processes (Akers, 1985; Hollinger, 1988, 1991, 1992; Skinner & Fream, 1997).

Skinner and Fream (1997) tested the relationship between the theoretical elements of social learning and the behaviors of cyber-criminals. The researchers (1997) posited that the nature of computer crime requires that individuals learn not only how to operate computer equipment, but also master specific procedures, programming, and techniques for using the computer for illegal activities. The researchers

(1997) examined five types of computer criminal activities for verifying this argument: (a) knowingly using, making, or giving to another person a "pirated" copy of commercially sold computer software; (b) trying to guess another's password to get into his or her computer account or files; (c) accessing another's computer account or files without his or her knowledge or permission just to look at the information or files; (d) adding, deleting, changing, or printing any information in another's computer files without the owner's knowledge or permission; and (e) writing or using a program that would destroy someone's computerized data (e.g., a virus, logic bomb, or Trojan horse).

The results of a multivariate regression analysis support social learning theory as an explanation for computer crime in general (Skinner & Fream, 1997). Skinner and Fream (1997) found that one of the most significant predictors of committing computer crime is interacting with friends who engage in illegal activities. If a student wants to learn how to use a computer for illegal activities, his friends, who have successful experience in these activities, are likely to offer advice and assistance. Friends are also generally willing to share technical information and allow others to acknowledge new-found games, programs, or techniques.

Skinner and Fream (1997) also found that family members significantly influence students' learning about the behavior of pirating software. Siblings and parents often distribute illegal copies of new programs and games in the family setting, if they have access to them. Interestingly, the research findings indicated that teachers who not only ignored piracy but who also strongly support it through their words and actions increased the frequency of piracy and violation of any type of computer crime among students (1997).

Guided by social learning theory and research, the proposed program can be driven upon the experience of empirically-validated school based-crime prevention programs. The primary goal of the computer prevention program is to facilitate the acquisition of solid ethical standards for general students, computer science students and computer professionals to acquire before they become cyber-criminals. The school is the setting for initial exposure and training in ethics, but the process is expected to continue in the workplace. The researcher suggests a potentially efficient strategy to deter future cyber-crimes through a well constructed computer ethics program. Ethics programs have been broadly utilized in various fields in our society. Most law enforcement training in the United States includes ethics training in order to provide "a clear definition of proper and improper conduct; mechanisms for detecting and sanctioning improper conduct" (Kappeler, 1998, pp. 216-217). Colleges and universities in the United States have Institutional Review Boards (IRB) in order to ensure that research is conducted in an ethical manner.

Computer professional associations such as the Association for Computing Machinery (ACM) and Association of Information Technology Professionals (AITP) have codes of ethics that establish expected behaviors and responsibilities for computer users and computer professionals (Harris, 2000, p. 1). Their codes of ethics share three major principles: "1) to maintain competence, 2) to disclose conflict of interest, and 3) to maintain confidentiality of information" (Harris, 2000, p. 1). The codes of ethics also contain sufficient ethical guidelines and regulations for computing practices. These codes of ethics, however, do not have any legal weight since both AITP and ACM are private membership organizations (Harris, 2000). Therefore, abiding by computer ethics becomes optional for computer users, and this option facilitates opportunities for computer crime and abuse (Harris, 2000). A mandated computer ethics program, followed by continuing reinforcement, is necessary to instill and maintain, within the next generation of computer users, appropriate guidelines for cyber behaviors.

Thus, establishing the mandated ethics program is vital for constructing pro-social views of cyber-crime among students. The sixth proposition of differential association states that individuals become criminals as the result of an excess of definitions favorable to violating the law over definitions unfavorable to violating the law (Sutherland, 1947). If individuals repeatedly observe that illegal computer activities are beneficial to them or others, they are more likely to engage in those activities.

In addition, computer ethics classes must address law and regulations relating to cyber-crime. Akers (1985) posited that social behavior responds to rewards and punishments. Any given behavior is likely to continue or to increase if it is followed by more rewards than punishments (Akers, 2004). The theory proposes that criminal and delinquent behavior is acquired, repeated, and changed by the same process as conforming behavior. In other words, when individuals observe more punishments than rewards, through consequences of their actions, they will likely discontinue the specific behaviors.

Instruction should include studies of court cases and convictions of cyber-crime from the Department of Justice. In addition, the class will examine existing government legislation on cyber-crime. By examining criminal law and court cases, students will understand the potential negative consequences of engaging in cyber-crime. One example of course content is listed below:

> In the fall of 1998, Congress passed the Identity Theft and Assumption Deterrence Act. This legislation made identity theft a new federal offense and prohibited:
> Knowingly transfer[ring] or us[ing], without lawful authority, a means of identification of another person with the intent to commit, or to aid or abet, any unlawful activity that constitutes a violation of Federal law, or that constitute a felony under any applicable State or local law (18 U.S.C. #1028[a][7]). Under general most circumstances, the offense carries a maximum term of 15 years' imprisonment, a fine, and criminal forfeiture of any personal property used or intended to be used in committing the offense or gained through the offense (Benner, 2000).

Social learning theorists hold that the learning process depends on priority, intensity, and duration (Akers, 2004). Skinner and Fream (1997) assert that the more college students associate with peers who are engaging in illegal computer activity, the greater the frequency of the behavior. The three tenets of the social learning process, priority, intensity, and duration, are the crucial elements in the proposed mandated ethics program. The proposed mandated ethics program should be implemented in the first year of college, followed by multiple training sessions before and after employees formally initiate their profession. In this way, the ethics course will be a more effective method to prevent computer crime. In addition, after graduation from college, students will naturally receive reinforcement through professional training sessions after they are hired by a company. Thus, the proposed ethical training should continue during the transition from college to the professional training setting, and would continue to increase and reinforce individuals' ethical standards.

The mandated ethics program is intended to intervene before individuals associate with new peers who encourage them to engage in illegal computer activities. Through the social learning process, individuals will eventually recognize the importance of abiding by ethical standards, policies, and procedures for computer usage as a student and computer professional. Furthermore, the mandated ethics course should change an individual's beliefs and attitudes so that they do not develop positive definitions about computer crime. In sum, when the future computer crime prevention program truly take both routine activities theoretical perspectives and the components of social learning perspectives into consideration, positive effects should be expected.

This book is an initial step toward constructing a solid computer-crime victimization model based on routine activities theory. In this study, routine activities theory is presented in detail in the main body of this study, via the combination of Hindelang et al.'s (1978) lifestyle-exposure theory and Cohen and Felson's (1979) routine activities theory.

The research has accomplished most of its main objectives. The main contribution of this research is that it constitutes an inventive attempt to uncover computer crime victimization by integrating two criminological victimization theories with the empirical assessment of SEM. From lifestyle-exposure theory, the research transformed from its crucial theoretical component, individual's daily living patterns, to individual's computer oriented lifestyle in cyberspace as one of main tenet in the model. From the perspective of routine activities theory, the crucial key element of a capable guardian was logically reconstructed with digital capable guardian, which represents computer security in this research.

The logical underpinning of the research has conveyed adequate empirical validity. The results of my empirical assessment demonstrate that online lifestyle and digital guardianship are all important aspects of a model delineating patterns of computer crime victimization. The analysis also yields very interesting results by indicating that demographic factors (race, age, and gender) differentially contribute to the levels of computer crime victimization, online lifestyle, and digital guardianship.

However, more efforts need to be done to build a more fully developed model. Despite of facts that most variables demonstrated adequate results, one of the major online lifestyle variables, computer security management, was unable to be tested in the model due to the low communality and reliability. In addition, one of significant potential factors derived from routine activities theory, computer criminals' motivation, was considered as a given situation.

In the future, the researcher hopes to develop more precise multimeasures of the central construct based on computer security and online lifestyle based on the theoretical components. Furthermore, adding computer criminals' motivational factors with a more refined measurement model reflecting these considerations stated in the previous section would substantially contribute to delineating true computer-crime victimization.

Presurvey Guideline

The following information will be necessary for you to know if you choose to participate in the upcoming survey. Please take the time to read and answer the following questions for your own personal knowledge. This information will assist you in accurately completing the actual survey. You may, and are encouraged, to bring this completed form with you for assistance during the actual survey.

Please refer to the software on your computer for assistance in answering the following questions:

Instructions: Please CHECK and, if applicable, WRITE your answer for each question.

For the following questions, please note that:

An antivirus program monitors a PC or laptop for computer viruses that might have gained access through an infected e-mail message, a music download, or an infected floppy disk (Moore, 2005). If the antivirus computer software locates a virus, the software will attempt to remove it, or to isolate it, so the virus cannot continue to be a threat to the computer system. The most efficient antivirus programs constantly monitor your computer, scan incoming and outgoing e-mails, and run complete scans every day (Moore, 2005).

Examples: Norton Antivirus, MacAfee Antivirus, Kaspersky Antivirus, etc.

During the last 10 months, did you have antivirus software on your personal, or laptop, computer?
    [   ] Yes
    [   ] No
    [   ] Don't own a personal, or laptop, computer

If you answered "Yes" to the question above, what type of antivirus software did you have on your computer?
    [   ] Kaspersky Antivirus
    [   ] McAfee Antivirus
    [   ] Norton/Symantec Antivirus
    [   ] Trend Micro Antivirus
    [   ] Zone Alarm Antivirus
    [   ] Other _____

For the following questions, please note that:

Antispyware computer software is designed to prevent spyware from being installed in the computer system. Spyware is a computer software that collects the online users' personal information without gaining their informed consent (Ramasastry, June 3, 2004, p. 1). Spyware may collect various types of information. Some spyware attempts to track the Web sites a user visits and then sends this information to an advertising agency. More malicious spyware attempts to intercept passwords or credit card numbers as a user enters into a Web form or other applications (Ramsastry, June 3, 2004, p. 13).

Examples: Trend Micro Antispyware, Ad-Aware SE Personal, Spybot, etc.

During the last 10 months, did you have antispyware software installed on your computer?

[　] Yes
[　] No
[　] Don't own a personal, or laptop, computer

If you answered "Yes" to the question above, what type of antispyware software did you have on your computer?

[　] Ad-Aware SE Personal
[　] McAfee Antispyware
[　] Norton Internet Security Antispyware
[　] Spybot
[　] Trend Micro Antispyware
[　] Windows Defender
[　] Other _____

For the following questions, please note that:

A firewall program prevents intruders from accessing your computer over the Internet or a local network. The most efficient firewalls allow you, on a case-by-case basis, to stop malicious programs that are already on your PC or laptop from connecting to the Internet. Moreover, firewalls may stop somebody from planting a virus, or worm, on your computer. However, firewalls do not detect or eliminate viruses. (Casey, 2000).

Example: ZoneAlarm Firewall, Norton Personal Firewall, etc.

During the last 10 months, did you have firewall software on your computer?
     [ ] Yes
     [ ] No
     [ ] Don't own a personal, or laptop, computer

If you answered "Yes" to the question above, what type of firewall software did you have on your computer?
     [ ] Lavasoft Personal Firewall
     [ ] McAfee Personal Firewall
     [ ] Norton/ Symantec Personal Firewall
     [ ] Pc-cillin Personal Firewall
     [ ] ZoneAlarm Firewall
     [ ] Windows XP Firewall
     [ ] Other _____

Computer Crime Victimization Survey

PLEASE ONLY PARTICIPATE IN THIS SURVEY IF YOU
OWN A PERSONAL, OR LAPTOP, COMPUTER!
All your responses must reflect your personal experience with your
own computer.

Part I
Instruction:
Please CHECK or WRITE your answer for each question.

A-1.
What is your gender?
   [   ] Male
   [   ] Female

A-2.
Age: _____ years old

A-3.
What is your race?
   [   ] African American
   [   ] Asian
   [   ] Caucasian

[   ] Hispanic
[   ] Native American
[   ] Other _____

A-4.

What is your class status?

[   ] Freshman
[   ] Sophomore
[   ] Junior
[   ] Senior

A-5.

Regarding the Internet, please mark the crime you most fear? **(Pick One)**

[   ] Internet Fraud: internet auction fraud and unsolicited e-mail
[   ] Identity Theft: stealing your social security number or credit card numbers
[   ] Hacking: virus infections and penetration of computer systems
[   ] Online Stalking
[   ] Cyber-harassment
[   ] Other: Please List: _____

A-6.

I know how to report to the police or government agencies if I become a victim of computer crime.

[   ] Yes
[   ] No

A-7.

During the last 10 months, did you use your own private personal, or laptop, computer?

[   ] Yes
[   ] No

NOTE: If you answer 'No' to this question, please stop
here and wait for the other students to finish their survey.

A-7-1.
During the last 10 months, how many months did you own your
personal, or laptop, computer?
_____ Months

A-8.
During the last 10 months did you use a school-owned computer?
    [   ] Yes
    [   ] No

A-9.
Which computer did you use the most?
    [   ] Personal, or Laptop, Computer
    [   ] School Computer
    [   ] Both Equally

A-10.
Did you use your personal, or laptop, computer on the Internet at
any time during the last 10 months?
    [   ] Yes
    [   ] No

NOTE: If you answer 'No' to this question, please stop
here and wait for the other students to finish their survey.

A-11.
During the last 10 months did you have Internet access at your:

A-11-1. home/apartment?
    [   ] Yes
    [   ] No

A-11-2. dormitory?
[   ] Yes
[   ] No

A-12.

Where did you use the Internet the most during the last 10 months?
[   ] Home/Dormitory/Apartment
[   ] School computer lab
[   ] Friend's/Relative's house
[   ] Other _____

A-13.

During the last 10 months, on average, how many **days per week**
did you use your personal, or laptop, computer on the Internet?
_____Days

A-14.

During the last 10 months, on average, how many **hours per week**
did you use your personal, or laptop, computer on the Internet?
_____Hrs

A-15. During the last 10 months, on average, did you use the
Internet (Pick only one):
[   ] Mostly during the week: Monday through Thursday
[   ] Mostly during the weekend: Friday through Sunday
[   ] Equally throughout Monday through Sunday

For the following questions, please note that:
the word "*hack*" is defined as gaining unauthorized access to a
computer system and start to modify computer settings or change
computer files, or cause various technical problems in a computer
system.

the word "*computer virus*" is defined as any unwanted computer
code which damages your computer system or causes it to start
behaving in an erratic manner such as damaging your programs,
disabling your programs, deleting your files, or reformatting your
hard drive.

A-16.
Was your computer hacked during the last 10 months?
   [   ] Yes
   [   ] No

A-17.
Did you experience any computer virus during the last 10 months?
   [   ] Yes
   [   ] No

A-18.
How do you rate your computer skills?
   [   ] Beginner
   [   ] Intermediate
   [   ] Advanced
   [   ] Expert

A-19.
What was your most frequent use of the Internet during last 10 months? (Pick only one)
   [   ] School work
   [   ] Communicate with others/ e-mail and messenger
   [   ] Entertainment (listening to music or watching movies)
   [   ] Purchasing items
   [   ] Online Banking
   [   ] Other: _____

A-20.
How many items did you purchase via online shopping during last 10 months?
   _____Items

Part II
Instructions:
The format used in this part of the survey to record responses is known as a visual analog scale or a magnitude estimation scale.

After reading a question, locate the response line. The response line is a continuous line with a pair of descriptors located at each end. The descriptors offer a continuum for your response. For example, the response could range from "Strongly Disagree" with the question to "Strongly Agree" with the question, or anywhere in between the two descriptors.

Please read each item and then place a vertical line on the scale that indicates how
much you agree or disagree with the following statements.

For example:
I love ice cream.
(This example, as evidenced by the redline, indicates about a 90% agreement with this statement.)

    0%   **50%**   **100%**
Strongly Disagree _____|___ Strongly Agree

B-1. I frequently checked my e-mail during the last 10 months.

Strongly Disagree _____ Strongly Agree

B-2. I frequently used an instant messenger (e.g., MSN, AOL, etc.) to communicate with people during the last 10 months.

Strongly Disagree _____ Strongly Agree

B-3. I frequently spent time downloading materials from the Internet during the last 10 months.

Strongly Disagree _____ Strongly Agree

B-4. I frequently spent time shopping on the Internet during the last 10 months.

Strongly Disagree _____ Strongly Agree

B-5. I frequently spent time on the Internet to entertain myself during the last 10 months.

Strongly Disagree_____ Strongly Agree

B-6. I frequently spent time on the Internet for study purposes during the last 10 months.

Strongly Disagree _____ Strongly Agree

B-7. I frequently viewed or watched news on the Internet during the last 10 months.

Strongly Disagree _____ Strongly Agree

B-8. I frequently sent e-mails to people during the last 10 months.

Strongly Disagree _____ Strongly Agree

B-9. I frequently spent time on the Internet when I was bored during the last 10 months.

Strongly Disagree _____ Strongly Agree

B-10. I frequently visited Web sites that were new to me during the last 10 months.

Strongly Disagree _____ Strongly Agree

B-11. I frequently visited social networking Web sites such as myspace.com during the last 10 months.

Strongly Disagree _____ Strongly Agree

B-12. I frequently downloaded free games from any Web site during the last 10 months.

Strongly Disagree _____ Strongly Agree

B-13. I frequently downloaded free music that interested me from any Web site during the last 10 months.

Strongly Disagree _____ Strongly Agree

B-14. I frequently downloaded free movies that interested me from any Web site during the last 10 months.

Strongly Disagree _____ Strongly Agree

B-15. I frequently opened any attachment in the e-mails that I received during the last 10 months.

Strongly Disagree _____ Strongly Agree

B-16. I frequently clicked on any Web-links in the e-mails that I received during the last 10 months.

Strongly Disagree _____ Strongly Agree

B-17. I frequently opened any file or attachment I received through my instant messenger during the last 10 months.

Strongly Disagree _____ Strongly Agree

B-18. I frequently clicked on a pop-up message that interested me during the last 10 months.

Strongly Disagree _____Strongly Agree

B-19. I frequently updated my computer security software during the last 10 months.

Strongly Disagree _____ Strongly Agree

B-20. I frequently changed the passwords for my e-mail accounts during the last 10 months.

Strongly Disagree _____ Strongly Agree

B-21. I used different passwords and user IDs for each of my Internet accounts during the last 10 months.

Strongly Disagree _____ Strongly Agree

B-22. I frequently checked to make sure my computer security software was on before I used the Internet during the last 10 months.

Strongly Disagree _____ Strongly Agree

B-23. I frequently searched for more effective computer security software during the last 10 months.

Strongly Disagree _____ Strongly Agree

B-24. I believed that my present computer security system was effective during the last 10 months.

Strongly Disagree _____ Strongly Agree

Part III

For the purpose of this part (Part III), you are provided with the following definitions to help you distinguish between Antivirus software, Spy-ware software, and Firewall software.

ANTIVIRUS SOFTWARE

An antivirus program monitors a PC or laptop for computer viruses that might have gained access through an infected e-mail message, a music download, or an infected floppy disk (Moore, 2005). If the antivirus computer software locates a virus, the software will attempt to remove it, or to isolate it, so the virus cannot continue to be a threat to the computer system. The most efficient antivirus programs constantly monitor your computer, scan incoming and outgoing e-mails, and run complete scans every day (Moore, 2005).

Examples: Norton Antivirus, MacAfee Antivirus, Kaspersky Antivirus, etc.

ANTISPYWARE SOFTWARE

Antispyware computer software is designed to prevent spyware from being installed in the computer system. Spyware is a computer software that collects the online users' personal information without gaining their informed consent (Ramasastry, June 3, 2004,:p. 1). Spyware may collect various types of information. Some spyware attempts to track the Web sites a user visits and then sends this information to an advertising agency. More malicious spyware attempts to intercept passwords or credit card numbers as a user enters into a Web form or other applications (Ramsastry, June 3, 2004,:p. 13).

Examples: Trend Micro Antispyware, Ad-Aware SE Personal, Spybot, etc.

FIREWALL SOFTWARE

A firewall program prevents intruders from accessing your computer over the Internet or a local network. The most efficient firewalls allow you, on a case-by-case basis, to stop malicious programs that are already on your PC or laptop from connecting to the Internet. Moreover, firewalls may stop somebody from planting a virus, or worm, on your computer. However, firewalls do not detect or eliminate viruses. (Casey, 2000).

Example: ZoneAlarm Firewall, Norton Personal Firewall, etc.

Please CHECK your answer for each question.

Cyber-security Knowledge Questions: True or False

C-1-1. Firewalls normally detect or eliminate viruses.
[   ] True
[   ] False

C-1-2. Spyware can intercept passwords or credit card numbers as a user enters them into a Web form or other application.
[   ] True
[   ] False

C-1-3. Antivirus computer software locates a virus, the software will attempt to remove it, or to isolate it, so the virus cannot continue to be a threat to the computer system.
[   ] True
[   ] False

C-1-4. A Firewall program blocks intruders from accessing your PC over the Internet or a local network.
[   ] True
[   ] False

Instructions: Please CHECK and, if applicable, WRITE your answer for each question.

AS A REMINDER

An antivirus program monitors a PC or laptop for computer viruses that might have gained an access through an infected e-mail message, a music download, or an infected floppy disk (Moore, 2005). If the antivirus computer software locates a virus, the software will attempt to remove it, or to isolate it, so the virus cannot continue to be a threat to the computer system. The most efficient antivirus programs constantly monitor your computer, scan incoming and outgoing e-mails, and run complete scans every day (Moore, 2005).

Examples: Norton Antivirus, MacAfee Antivirus, Kaspersky

Antivirus, etc.

C-2-1. Did you have antivirus software on your computer during the last 10 months?

     [   ] Yes
     [   ] No

C-2-2. If you answered "Yes" to the question above, what type of antivirus software did you have on your computer during the last 10 months?

     [   ] Kaspersky Antivirus
     [   ] McAfee Antivirus
     [   ] Norton/Symantec Antivirus
     [   ] Trend Micro Antivirus
     [   ] Zone Alarm Antivirus
     [   ] Other _____

Please read the item below and then place a vertical line on the scale that indicates how much you agree or disagree with the following statement.

C-2-3. I always had antivirus software on my computer during the last 10 months.

Strongly Disagree _____ Strongly Agree

AS A REMINDER

Antispyware computer software is designed to prevent spyware from being installed in the computer system. Spyware is a computer software that collects the online users' personal information without gaining their informed consent (Ramasastry, June 3, 2004, p. 1). Spyware may collect various types of information. Some spyware attempts to track the Web sites a user visits and then sends this information to an advertising agency. More malicious spyware attempts to intercept passwords or credit card numbers as a user enters into a Web form or other applications (Ramsastry, June 3, 2004, p. 13).

Examples: *Trend Micro Antispyware, Ad-Aware SE Personal, Spybot, etc.*

C-3-1. Did you have antispyware software on your computer during the last 10 months?

[   ] Yes
[   ] No

C-3-2. If you answered "Yes" to the question above, what type of antispyware software did you have on your computer during the last 10 months?

[   ] Ad-Aware SE Personal
[   ] McAfee Antispyware
[   ] Norton Internet Security Antispyware
[   ] Spybot
[   ] Trend Micro Antispyware
[   ] Windows Defender
[   ] Other _____

Please read the item below and then place a vertical line on the scale that indicates how much you agree or disagree with the following statement.

C-3-3. I always had antispyware software on my computer during the last 10 months.

Strongly Disagree _____ Strongly Agree

AS A REMINDER

A firewall program prevents intruders from accessing your computer over the Internet or a local network. The most efficient firewalls allow you, on a case-by-case basis, to stop malicious programs that are already on your PC or laptop from connecting to the Internet. Moreover, firewalls may stop somebody from planting a virus, or worm, on your computer. However, firewalls do not detect or eliminate viruses. (Casey, 2000).

Example: ZoneAlarm Firewall, Norton Personal Firewall, etc.

C-4-1. Did you have firewall software on your computer during the last 10 months?
      [   ] Yes
      [   ] No

C-4-2. If you answered "Yes" to the question above, what type of firewall software did you have on your computer during the last 10 months?
      [   ] Lavasoft Personal Firewall
      [   ] McAfee Personal Firewall
      [   ] Norton/ Symantec Personal Firewall
      [   ] Pc-cillin Personal Firewall
      [   ] ZoneAlarm Firewall
      [   ] Windows XP Firewall
      [   ] Other _____

Please read the item below and then place a vertical line on the scale that indicates how much you agree or disagree with the following statement.

C-4-3. I always had firewall software on my computer during the last 10 months.

Strongly Disagree _____ Strongly Agree

Part IV
Instructions: Please CHECK or WRITE your answer for each question.

For the following questions,
the word *"computer virus"* is defined as **any unwanted computer code which destroys files or your computer system or causes start having problems**

D-1. During the last 10 months, did you experience a computer virus infection?
  [   ] Yes
  [   ] No
  [   ] Don't Know

D-2. During the last 10 months, how many times did you have computer virus infection incidents?
  _____ Times

D-3. During the last 10 months, approximately how much money did you spend on the computer security programs such as antivirus, firewalls, antispyware, etc? (if you did not spend any money, put 0)
  _____ Dollars

D-4. During the last 10 months, approximately how much money did you spend fixing your computer due to computer virus infections? (if you did not spend any money, put 0)
  _____ Dollars

D-5. During the last 10 months, approximately how many hours were spent fixing your computer due to the virus infections?
  _____ Hours

D-6. During the last 10 months, how many of the computer virus infection incidents did you report to law enforcement agencies? (if you did not report any computer virus infection to law enforcement agencies, put 0)

_____ Times

D-7. During the last 10 months, how many of the computer virus infection incidents did you report to computer software or manufacturing companies (e.g., Dell, Gateway, Microsoft, Norton, etc.)? (If you did not report any computer virus infection to the private companies, put 0)

_____ Times

Computer Crime Victimization Survey (Set II)

During the last 10 months, if you used a public computer in addition to your personal, or laptop computer, please complete the following portions of this survey. All your responses here must reflect your personal experience in the usage of public computers only.

Part I
Instruction:
Please CHECK or WRITE your answer for each question.

E-1.
Did you use a public computer such as a school computer in the computer lab or a Cyber-café computer during the last 10 months?

[   ] Yes
[   ] No

NOTE: If you answer 'No' to this question, please stop here and wait for the other students to finish their survey.

E-2.
Did you use a public computer on the Internet during the last 10 months?

    [   ] Yes
    [   ] No

NOTE: If you answer 'No' to this question, please stop here and wait for the other students to finish their survey.

Part II
Instructions:
This portion of the survey is designed to assist you in accurately indicating your responses. The format used in this survey to record responses is known as a visual analog scale or a magnitude estimation scale.

After reading a question, locate the response line. The response line is a continuous line with a pair of descriptors located at each end. The descriptors offer a continuum for your response. For example, the response could range from "Strongly Disagree" with the question to "Strongly Agree" with the question, or anywhere in between the two responses.

Please read each item and then place ONLY ONE VERTICAL LINE on the scale that indicates how much you agree or disagree with the following statements.

For example:
I love ice cream.
(This example, as evidenced by the redline, indicates about a 90% agreement with this statement.)

    0%   **50%**   **100%**
Strongly Disagree _____|___ Strongly Agree

E-1. I frequently checked my e-mail using a public computer during the last 10 months.

Strongly Disagree _____ Strongly Agree

E-2. I frequently used an instant messenger (e.g., MSN, AOL, etc.) on a public computer to communicate with people during the last 10 months.

Strongly Disagree _____ Strongly Agree

E-3. I frequently spent time downloading materials on a public computer from the Internet during the last 10 months.

Strongly Disagree _____ Strongly Agree

E-4. I frequently spent time shopping on the Internet using a public computer during the last 10 months.

Strongly Disagree _____ Strongly Agree

E-5. I frequently spent time on the Internet using a public computer to entertain myself during the last 10 months.

Strongly Disagree_____ Strongly Agree

E-6. I frequently spent time on the Internet using a public computer for study purposes during the last 10 months.

Strongly Disagree _____ Strongly Agree

E-7. I frequently viewed or watched news on the Internet using a public computer during the last 10 months.

Strongly Disagree _____ Strongly Agree

E-8. I frequently sent e-mails using a public computer to people during the last 10 months.

Strongly Disagree _____ Strongly Agree

E-9. I frequently spent time on the Internet using a public computer when I was bored during the last 10 months.

Strongly Disagree _____ Strongly Agree

E-10. I frequently visited Web sites that were new to me using a public computer during the last 10 months.

Strongly Disagree _____ Strongly Agree

E-11. I frequently visited social networking Web sites such as myspace.com using a public computer during the last 10 months.

Strongly Disagree _____ Strongly Agree
E-12. I frequently downloaded free games from any Web site using a public computer during the last 10 months.

Strongly Disagree _____ Strongly Agree

E-13. I frequently downloaded free music from any Web site using a public computer during the last 10 months.

Strongly Disagree _____ Strongly Agree

E-14. I frequently downloaded free movies from any Web site using a public computer during 2006 the last 10 months.

Strongly Disagree _____ Strongly Agree

E-15. I frequently opened any attachment in the e-mails that I received using a public computer during the last 10 months.

Strongly Disagree _____ Strongly Agree

E-16. I frequently clicked on any Web-links in the e-mails that I received using a public computer during the last 10 months.

Strongly Disagree _____ Strongly Agree

E-17. I frequently opened any file or attachment I received through my instant messenger using a public computer during the last 10 months.

Strongly Disagree _____ Strongly Agree

E-18. I frequently clicked on a pop-up message that interested me using a public computer during the last 10 months.

Strongly Disagree _____ Strongly Agree

E-19. I frequently updated the computer security software on any public computer I was using during the last 10 months.

Strongly Disagree _____ Strongly Agree

E-20. I frequently changed the passwords for my e-mail accounts using a public computer during the last 10 months.

Strongly Disagree _____ Strongly Agree

E-21. I used different passwords and user IDs for each of my Internet accounts while using a public computer during the last 10 months.

Strongly Disagree _____ Strongly Agree

E-22. I frequently checked to make sure the public computer security software was on before I used the Internet during the last 10 months.

Strongly Disagree _____ Strongly Agree

E-23. I frequently searched for more effective computer security software while using a public computer during the last 10 months.

Strongly Disagree _____ Strongly Agree

E-24. I believed that the computer security system on the public computer I used during the last 10 months was effective.

Strongly Disagree _____ Strongly Agree

Part III
Instructions: the following is a two part question

> **Part 1)**
> **Please read the item below and then place ONLY ONE
> VERTICAL LINE on the scale that indicates how much you
> agree or disagree with the following statement.**
>
> **Part 2)**
> **Then, please provide a brief explanation of your answer in the
> box that immediately follows your response line answer.**

Part 1)
I feel more comfortable using public computers when visiting unknown
Web sites than using my own computer

Strongly Disagree _____ Strongly Agree

Part 2)

Please explain Why you DO or DO NOT feel more comfortable using a public computer for this purpose.

References

2002 Internet fraud report. (2003). Retrieved June 1, 2007, from http://www .ic3.gov/media/annualreports.aspx

2004 Australian computer crime and security survey. (2005). Retrieved June 1, 2007, from http://www.auscert.org.au/render.html?it=2001

2004 IC3 Internet crime report. (2005). Retrieved June 1, 2007, from http://www .ic3.gov/media/annualreports.aspx

2005 FBI computer crime survey. (2006). Retrieved November 6, 2006, from http://www.fbi.gov/publications/ccs2005.pdf

2008 Computer Crime & Security Survey. (2009). Retrieved September1, 2009, from http://www.atl-htcia.org/files/csi2008.pdf

2008 IC3 Internet crime report. (2009). Retrieved September1, 2009, from http://www.ic3.gov/media/2009/090331.aspx

Adams, P. (1998). Network topologies and virtual place. *Annals of Association of American Geographers, 88*(1), 88-106.

Anderson, M. (1997). In the computer age, law enforcement agencies face new challenges and risks. *Justice & Technology*. Retrieved November 20, 2004, from http://www.govtech.net/magazine/gt/1997/feb/feb97-jandt/feb97-jandt.php

Akers, R (1997). Criminological theories: Introduction and evaluation (2nd ed.). Los Angeles: Roxbury.

Bachman, R., & Paternoster., R (2004). *Statistics for Criminology and Criminal justice*. New York: McGraw-Hill Companies, Inc.

Barak, G. (1995). *Media, process, and the social construction of crime.* New York: Garland.

Bennett, R. (1991). Routine activities: A cross-national assessment of a criminological perspective. *Social Forces 70*(1), 147-163.

Bernburg, J. G., & Thorlindsson, T. (2001). Routine activities in social context: A closer look at the role of opportunity in deviant behavior. *Justice Quarterly, 18*, 543-567.

Birkbeck, C., & LaFree, G. (1993). The situational analysis of crime and deviance. *Annual Review of Sociology 19*(2), 113-37.

Bolgona, G. J., & Lindquist, R. J. (1987). *Fraud auditing and forensic accounting.* New York: John Wiley..

Britz, M. T. (2004). *Computer forensics and cyber crime.* New Jersey: Pearson Prentice Hall.

Carter, L. D., & Katz, J. A. (1997). *Computer crime: An emerging challenge for law enforcement.* Retrieved November 20, 2004, from http://www.sgrm.com/ art11.htm

Casey, E. (2000). *Digital evidence and computer crime.* London: Academic Press.

Castells, M. (2002). *The internet galaxy: Reflections on the Internet, business, and society.* Oxford, United Kingdom: Oxford University Press.

Chatterton, M. R., & Frenz, S. J. (1994) Closed-circuit television: Its role in reducing burglaries and the fear of crime in sheltered accommodation for the elderly. *Security Journal, 5*(3), 133-139

Chou, C. P., & Bentler, P. M. (1995). Estimates and test in structural equation modeling. In R. H. Hoyle (Ed.), *Structural equation modeling: Concepts, issues, and applications* (pp. 37-54). Thousand Oaks, CA: Sage.

Clarke, R. V. (Ed.) (1992) *Situational crime prevention: Successful case studies.* Albany, NY: Harrow and Heston.

Clarke, R. V., & Homel, R. (1997) A revised classification of situational crime prevention techniques. In S. P. Lab (Ed.), *Crime prevention at the crossroads* (pp.17-30). Cincinnati, OH: Anderson.

Cohen, L. E., & Cantor, D. (1980). The determinants of larceny: An empirical and theoretical study. *Journal of Research in Crime and Delinquency, 17*(1), 140-159.

Corrado, R., Roesch, R., Glackman, W., Evans J., & Leger, G. (1980). Lifestyles and personal victimization: A test of the model with Canadian survey data. *Journal of Crime and Justice 3*(1), 125-149.

Cohen, L. E., & Felson, M. (1979). Social change and crime rate trends: A routine activity approach. *American Sociological Review, 44*, 588-608

Cohen, L. E., Felson, M., & Land, K. (1981). Social inequality and predatory criminal victimization: An exposition and a test of a formal theory. *American Sociological Review, 46*, 505-524.

Corrado, R., Roesch, R., Glackman, W., Evans, J., & Leger, G. (1980). Lifestyles and personal victimization: A test of the model with Canadian survey Data, *Journal of Crime and Justice, 3,* 125-149.

Darlington, R. (2004). *Factor Analysis* Retrieved January 08, 2008, from http://www.psych.cornell.edu/Darlington/factor.htm

Denning, D. (1999). *Information warfare and security.* Boston: Addison Wesley.

DeVellis, R. (2004). *Scale development.* London: Sage.

Docherty (Producer). (2001). *Hackers* [Motion picture]. (Available from PBS Video, PO BOX 609 Melbourne, FL, 32902-0609).

Dodge, M. (1990). *City of quartz: Excavating the future of Los Angeles.* London: Verso.

Duke, D. L. (1989). School organization, leadership, and student behavior. In O.C. Moles (Ed.), *Strategies to Reduce Student Misbehavior* (pp. 19-46). Washington, DC: US Department of Education.

Eck, J. (1995). Examining routine activity theory: A review of two books. *Justice Quarterly, 12,*783-797.

Erdfelder, E., Faul, F., & Buchner, A. (1996). GPOWER: A general power analysis program. *Behavior Research Methods, Instruments, & Computers, 28*(1), 1-11.

Etter, B. (2001). *The forensic challenges of e-crime, current commentary No.3.* Adelaide, Australia: Australasian centre for Policing Research.

Elliot, D., Huizinga, D., & Ageton, S. (1985). *Explaining delinquency and drug use.* Beverly Hills, CA: Sage.

Flanagan, W., & McMenamin, B. (1992). The playground bullies are learning to type, *Forbes, 150,* 184-189.   Retrieved February 6, 2007. from http://www.mindvox .com/cgi-bin/WebObjects/MindVoxUI.woa/wa/staticpage%

Felson, M. (1986). Routine activities, social controls, rational decisions and criminal outcomes. In D. Cornish and R. Clarke (Eds) *The reasoning criminal* (pp. 302-327). New York: Springer Verlag.

Felson, M. (1998). *Crime and everyday life: Insights and implications for society,* (2nd ed.). Thousand Oaks, CA: Pine Forge Press.

Fowler, F. (2002). *Survey research methods.* Beverly Hill, CA: Sage.

Furnell, S. (2002). *Cybercrime: Vandalizing the information society.* London: Addison Wesley.

Garofalo, J. (1987). Reassessing the lifestyle model of criminal victimization. In M Gottfredson & T. Hirschi (Eds.), *Positive criminology* (pp. 23-42). San Francisco: Sage.

Gibbs, J. J., Giever, D., & Higgins, G. E. (2003). A test of the Gottfredson and Hirschi general theory of crime using structural equation modeling. *Criminal Justice and Behavior, 30,* 441-458.

Giever, D. (1995). *An empirical assessment of the core elements of Gottfredson and Hirschi's general theory of crime.* Unpublished doctoral book, Indiana University of Pennsylvania, Indiana, PA.

Goldstein, A. (1994). *The ecology of aggression.* New York: Plenum Press

Gordon, M. P., Loef, M. P., Lucyshyn, W., & Richardson, R. (2004). *CSI/FBI computer crime and security survey.* Los Angeles: Computer Security Institute.

Gottfredson, M. R. (1984). *Victims of crime: The dimensions of risk. Home Office Research Study No.18..* London: Her Majesty's Stationer.

Gottfredson, M. R. (1986). Substantive contributions of victimization surveys. In Michael Tonry & Norval Morris (Eds.), *Crime and justice: An annual review of research,.* Chicago: University of Chicago Press.

Gottfredson, D. C., Gerstenblith, S. A., Soule, D. A., Womer, S. C., & Lu, S. (2004). Do afterschool programs prevent delinquency? *Prevention Science, 4,* 253-266.

Gottfredson, D. C., Gottfredson, G D., & Hybl, L. G, (1993). Managing adolescent behavior: A multiyear, multischool study. *American Educational Research Journal, 30*(1), 179-215.

Gover, A. R. (2004). Risky lifestyles and dating violence: A theoretical test of violent victimization. *Journal of Criminal Justice 32*(2), 171-180.

Grabosky, P. (2000, March). *Cyber crime and information warfare.* Paper presented at the Transnational Crime Conference convened by the Australian Institute of Criminology in association with the Australian Federal Police and Australian Customs Service.

Grabosky, P., & Smith, R. (2001). Telecommunication fraud in the digital age: The convergence of technologies. In D. Wall (Ed.) Crime and the Internet. London: Routledge.

Hidelang, M. J., Gottfredson, M. R., & Gaffalo, J. (1978). *Victims of personal crime: An empirical foundation for a theory of personal victimization.* Cambridge, MA: Ballinger.

Higgins, G. (2001). *Gottfredson and Hirschi's general theory of crime: A structural equation modeling approach.* Unpublished doctoral book, Indiana University of Pennsylvania, Indiana, PA.

Hinduja, S. (2010). Criminal Justice and Cyberspace. In G. Higgins (Eds.), *Cybercrime* (pp. 133-150). New York: McGraw-Hill.

Hoffer, J. A., & Straub, D. W. (1989). The 9 to 5 underground: Are you policing computer crimes. *Sloan Management Review, 30*(4), 35-44

Holt, T. (2009). Lone hacks or group cracks: Examining the social organization of computer hackers. In F. Schmalleger and M. Pittaro (Eds.), *Crimes of the Internet* (pp. 336-355). New Jersey: Pearson.

Hu, L., & Bentler, P. M. (1995). Evaluating model fit. In R. H. Hoyle (Ed.), *Structural equation modeling: Concepts, issues, and applications* (pp. 76-99). Thousand Oaks, CA: Sage..

Internet Fraud Complaint Center. (2003). *IFCC 2002 Internet fraud report.* Washington, DC: U.S. Government Printing Office.

Jesilow, P., Klempner, E., & Chiao, V. (1992). Reporting consumer and major fraud. In K. Schlegel & D. Weisburd (Eds.), *White collar crime: Issues and research* (pp. 149-168). Boston: Northeastern University Press.

Johnston, R. (2002). The battle against white-collar crime: The exponential growth of technology and the use of computers have triggered a purposeful rethinking of the tools needed by law enforcement organizations to address internet-related crime. *USA Today, 130,* pp. 36-39.

Joreskog, K., & Sorbom, D. (1996). *Lisrel 8: User's reference guide.* Chicago: Scientific Software Internal.

Kaplan, D. (2000). *Structural equation modeling: Foundations and extensions.* Thousand Oaks, CA: Sage.

Karmen, A. (2006). *Crime victims.* Thousand Oaks, CA: Thomson Higher Education

Kabay, M. E. (2001). *Studies and surveys of computer crime.* Norwich, CT: Department of Computer Information Systems.

Kennedy, L. W., & Forde, D. R. (1990). Routine activities and crime: An analysis of victimization in Canada. *Criminology* 28, 137-151.

Kim, J., & Mueller, C. (1978), Factor analysis: Statistical methods and practical issues. London: Sage.

Kline, R. B. (1998). *Principles and practices of structural equation modeling.* New York: Guildford Press.

Knetzger, M., & Muraski, J. (2008), *Investigating high-tech crime,* Upper Saddle River, NJ: Pearson.

Komorosky, D. (2003). *Predictors of rape myth acceptance among criminology and noncriminology students.* Unpublished doctoral dissertation, Indiana University of Pennsylvania, Indiana, PA

Kowalski, M. (2002). *Cyber-crime: Issues, data sources, and feasibility of collecting police-reported statistics.* Ottawa: Statistics Canada.

Kubic, T. (2001, May 23). *Internet fraud crime problems.* Washington, DC: Congressional Statement, Federal Bureau of Investigation.

Kubic, T. (2001, June 12). *The FBI's perspective on the cyber crime problems.* Washington, DC: Congressional Testimony, Federal Bureau of Investigation.

Laub, J. H. (1990). Patterns of criminal victimization in the United States. In A. J. Lurigio, W. G. Skogan, & R. C. Davis (Eds.), *Victims of crime: Problems, polices and programs.* Newbury Park, CA: Sage.

Laycock, G. (1985) *Property marking: A deterrent to domestic burglary?* London: Home Office.

Laycock, G. (1991) Operation identification, or the power of publicity? *Security Journal, 2*(3), 67-72.

Lewis-Beck, M. (1980). Applied regression: An introduction. Newbury Park, CA: Sage.

Loehlin, J. (1992). *Latent variable models: An introduction to factor, path, and structural analysis* (2nd ed.). Hillsdale, NJ: Lawrence Erlbaum.

Lynch, J. P. (1987). Routine activity and victimization at work. *Journal of Quantitative Criminology 3,* 283-300.

Massey, J., Krohn, M., & Bonati, L. (1989). Property crime and the routine activities of individuals. *Journal of Research in Crime and Delinquency 26,* 378-400.

Maxfield, M. G., & Babbie, E. (2005). *Research methods for criminal justice and criminology* (4th ed.). Belmont, CA: Thompson Wadsworth.

McConnell International LLC. (2000). *Cyber crime... and punishment? Archaic laws threaten global Information.* Washington, DC: McConnell International.

McQuade, S. C. (2006). *Understanding and managing cybercrime.* Boston:Pearson/Allyn and Bacon.

Miethe, T., & Meier, R. (1990). Criminal opportunity and victimization rates: A structural-choice theory of criminal victimization. *Journal of Research in Crime and Delinquency 27,* 243-266.

Miethe, T., Stafford, M., & Long, J. S. (1987). Social differentiation in criminal victimization: A test of routine activities/ lifestyle theories. *American Sociological Review 52*(2), 184-194.

Meier R., & Miethe, T. (1993). Understanding theories of criminal victimization. *Crime and Justice 17,* 459-499.

Mitchell, W. J. (1995). *City of bits: Space, place and the Infobahn.* Cambridge, MA: MIT Press.

Moitra, S. D. (2005) Developing policies for cyber crime. *European Journal of Crime, Criminal Law and Criminal Justice, 13*(3), 435-464

Moore, R. (2005). *Cybercrime: Investigating high-technology computer crime.* Philadelphia: LexisNexis Group.

Mustaine, E., & Tewksbury, R. (1998). Predicting risks of larceny theft victimization: A routine activity analysis using refined lifestyle measures. *Criminology 36*, 829-857.

New bug slowed by virus guards. (2000, May 20). *Winston-Salem Journal*, pp. A1:A11.

Osgood, D. W., Wilson, J. K., O'Malley, P. M., Bachman, J. G., & Johnston, L. D. (1996). Routine activities and individual deviant behavior. *American Sociological Review. 61*, 635-655.

Parker, D. B. (1998). *Fighting computer crime: A new framework for protecting information.* New York: Wiley.

Piazza, P. (2006, November). Technofile:Antisocial networking sites. *Security Management*, 1-5.

Poyner, B. (1991). Situational crime prevention in two parking facilities. *Security Journal, 2*, 96-101.

Ramasastry, A. (2004). *Cable News Network (CNN).com. Can Utah's new antispyware law work?* Retrieved January 16, 2007, from http://www.cnn.com/2004/ LAW/06/03/ramasastry.spyware/index.html

Rigdon, E. (1997). *Approaches to testing identification.* Retrieved January 11, 2006, from http://www.gsu .edu/~mkteer/identifi.html

Roncek, D. W., & Maier, P. A. (1991) Bars, blocks, and crimes revisited: Linking the theory of routine activities to the empiricism of hot spots. *Criminology, 29*, 725-753.

Rosenblatt, K. S. (1996), *High-technology crime.* San Jose, CA: KSK.

Sampson, R. J., & Woodredge, J. D. (1987). Linking the micro- and macro-level dimensions of lifestyle-routine activity and opportunity models of predatory victimization. *Journal of Quantitative Criminology, 3*, 371-393.

Schlegel, K., & Weisburd, D. (1992). White-collar crime: The parallax view. In K. Schlegel & D. Weisburd (Eds.), *White collar crime: Issues and research* (pp. 3-27). Boston: Northeastern University Press.

Schumcker, R. E., & Lomax, R. G. (1996). *A beginner's guide to structural equation modeling.* Mahwah, NJ: Lawrence Erlbaum.

Smith, S. J. (1982). Victimization in the inner city. *British Journal of Criminology, 22*(2), 386-402.

Sherman, L. W., Gartin, P. R., & Buerger, M. E. (1989). Hot spots of predatory crime: routine activities and the criminology of place. *Criminology, 27*(2), 27-55.

Stalder, F. (1998). *The logic of networks: Social landscapes vis-à-vis the space of flows.* Retrieved November 26, 2005, from http://www.ctheory.net/ text_file.asp?pick=263

Standler, B. R. (2002, September 4). *Computer crime.* Retrieved February 6, 2005, from http://www.rbs2.com/ccrime.htm

Stankom, E. A. (1995) Women, crime and fear. *Annuals of American Political and Social Science, 539,* 46-58.

Sutherland, E. (1947). *Principles of criminology* (4th ed.). New York: Harper & Row.

Taylor, W. R., Caeti, J. T., Loper, D. K., Fritsch, J. E., and Liederbach, J (2006). *Digital crime and digital terrorism.* New Jersey: Person Education.

Thomas, D., & Loader, B. (2000). Introduction–Cybercrime: Law enforcement, security and surveillance in the information age. In D. Thomas & B. Loader (Eds.), *Cybercrime: Law enforcement, security and surveillance in the information age.* London: Routledge.

Tiernan, B. (2000). *E-tailing.* Chicago: Dearborn.

Tilley, N. (1993b) *Understanding car parks, crime and CCTIV: Evaluation lessons from safer cities.* London: Home Office.

Tseloni, A., Witterbrood, K., Farrell, G., & Pease, K. (2004). Burglary victimization in England and Wales, the United States and The Netherlands: A cross-national comparative test of routine activities and lifestyle theories. *British Journal of Criminology 44*(1), 66-92.

U.S. Department of Justice. (1998, March 18). *Juvenile computer hacker cuts off FAA tower at regional airport.* Retrieved February 6, 2005, from http://www.usdoj .gov/criminal/cybercrime/juvenilepld.htm

Wark, M. (2010). Hackers. In G. Higgins (Eds.), *Cybercrime* (pp. 133-150). New York: McGraw-Hill.

Webb, B., & Laycock, G. (1992) *Reducing crime on the London underground: An evaluation of three pilot projects..* London: Home Office.

Williams, F. P., & McShane, M. D. (1999). *Criminological theory.* Upper Saddle River, NJ: Prentice Hall.

Yar, M. (2005). The novelty of 'cybercrime': An assessment in light of routine activity theory. *European Society of Criminology, 2,* 407-427.

York, R. O. (1998). *Conducting social work research: An experimental approach.* Needham Heights: Allyn & Bacon.

Index

.

CPSIA information can be obtained at www.ICGtesting.com
Printed in the USA
BVOW060405270212

283783BV00003B/5/P